The
White
Ladder
Diaries

The
White
Ladder
Diaries

The pain and pleasure of launching a business

Ros Jay
Editor: Richard Craze

new tricks for old dogs

Published by White Ladder Press Ltd
Great Ambrook, Near Ipplepen, Devon TQ12 5UL
01803 813343
www.whiteladderpress.com

First published in Great Britain in 2004

ISBN 0 9543914 1 1

British Library Cataloguing in Publication Data
A CIP record for this book can be obtained from the British Library.

Designed and typeset by Julie Martin Ltd
Cover design by Julie Martin Ltd
Printed and bound by TJ International Ltd, Padstow, Cornwall

White Ladder Press Ltd
Great Ambrook, Near Ipplepen, Devon TQ12 5UL
01803 813343
www.whiteladderpress.com

List of information panels

Acknowledgements

There are many people I'd like to thank in connection with this book. Not so much people who have helped with this book itself, but all those who helped with the subject of the book: the conception and launch of White Ladder Press.

To begin with, it is impossible to overemphasise (so I shan't try) the wisdom, support and help of our editorial board, who have cheerfully put up with constant pestering from us, and still do: Mark Allin, Elie Ball, Matthew Clarke, Tony Jay and Rachael Stock. I have no doubt whatever that without them, White Ladder Press wouldn't have stood a chance. They are an enviable panel of advisors, and a fantastic group of friends too.

We have also pestered a number of other people who have somehow managed to reveal no sign of frustration but always responded with great enthusiasm and plenty of good advice. I must mention in particular Susan Hill, whose experience in starting her own publishing company was hugely helpful to us; experience which she has shared generously. I also want to thank Sarah Clarke, Maggie Tree, Catherine Dawson, and John Cleese who endorsed our first book.

I can't quite believe how lucky we've been in finding some terrific suppliers (who feel more like partners than suppliers), many recommended by colleagues and advisors. Among them are Guy Courtney and his team at Pedalo who have given us a great website,

Julie Martin who manages to make our books stand out with her cover designs and typesetting, Allan Lovegrove at Alton Logistics, Deborah Jones at TJI Printing, Graham Howe, and Judy Hedger for her excellent photography.

I have restricted myself to thanking those people who were involved in the launch of White Ladder Press and our first book, *Kids & Co.* However I am also very grateful to all those people who have helped us since, many of whom we are still working with.

Finally I have to thank Rich, the other half of White Ladder Press, without whom there would be no book, no business, and not nearly so much fun either.

Disclaimer

This is a journal of our experiences setting up our own business. We cannot take responsibility for any legal information in here – as far as I know it's all accurate but please take professional advice if you need to be certain. As far as prices are concerned, they were accurate when the journal was written and many will still be correct. At least they should all give you a ball park figure. Much of the value of this book seems to me to lie in the immediacy of the real life experience as it happens. I think this would be lost if I went through updating all the figures. So I haven't.

Introduction

This is a personal story. It's the story of how Rich and I had more fun at work than we'd had for years – even though we were both already doing jobs we enjoyed. It's the story of how we went from being freelance writers working for other people to being publishers working for ourselves.

Starting our own business was something we'd both been thinking about for years. But we hadn't seen our chance before. Maybe we had at times, but we'd failed to make that leap from idea to reality. There'd always been a better reason for not making the jump than for making it: it would cost too much, we didn't know the market well enough, it probably wouldn't work. Our ideas had ranged from running a café to selling wall hangings, and even marketing a motorised pushchair.

In the end, though, we found the momentum we needed in a business far closer to home. For us, the switch from writing to publishing was huge and involved learning a mass of new information very fast. But in the grand scheme of things, it's not such a big jump as, say, from writing to manufacturing pushchairs.

Personally, I don't think I'd ever have made the jump without Rich to encourage me. And I doubt he'd have done it without me, either. I was nervous of a lot of the work involved. Not nervous of doing it, but of knowing where to start. The notion of starting a business filled me with thoughts of accounting systems, registering as a limited company, dealing with admin (I didn't know what that involved but it just sounded like something I wouldn't know how to do). This is probably a lot of what had deterred me in the past. All those other reasons for not starting businesses were just excuses, really, for not leaving a comfortable safe job and throwing myself into the unknown.

But Rich was completely unphased by all these things. He'd done most of it before, and what he hadn't, he was happy to learn. What intimidated him was the thought of getting to grips with marketing and sales. Here, however, I was on firm ground, and genuinely relished the prospect of having my own products to market. I'd done lots of work with small businesses helping them to market themselves more effectively, and I'd even written several books on the subject. Marketing was always my thing. That was the main reason I'd always wanted my own business, so I could enjoy the marketing (and prove along the way that I knew what I was talking about in the books I'd written).

So between us we had plenty of relevant experience, but also plenty of gaps in our knowledge too. Probably pretty much like you, and indeed anyone who is about to launch a business of their own.

Of course, the chances are you're not about to launch a publishing business. Maybe you're setting up a bicycle repair service, or growing herbs to sell to local restaurants and delicatessens. It doesn't much matter actually. This journal is about launching a small business, not running one, and most of the lessons are generic, so you'll find plenty of value here even if your business is completely unrelated to publishing. You might be selling dog beds by mail order or providing refrigerated transport to the wet fish industry.

For all new businesses, certain issues stand out. In our case, to give one example, we tortured ourselves (quite excessively as it turned out) over discounts. It was a crucial part of our pricing, as it is for many small businesses, and indeed large ones. In your case, the knotty problem might be sourcing suitable suppliers, designing the packaging or finding the right outlets. But following the thinking processes we went through, and observing how we went about resolving the question, sheds light on the approach you can take to all sorts of other issues. The fact is that we small businesses have a lot in common and we can all learn from each other, including each other's mistakes.

I hope you'll learn from ours. And you'll learn from the things we got right too. I've flagged up the golden rules we learnt along the way to make it easier for you to pick out the real essentials. You'll also find these summarised at the end. And I've passed on all sorts of useful facts and skills which we learned along the way, from how to register a limited company through to the information you need on your customer database.

On top of all the facts, skills and tips I've injected into this book, I've also chosen to reproduce the diary I kept, as I kept it, rather than write a textbook. I've done this because it seems to me that one of the biggest elements of starting a business is your own emotional input: your hopes, fears, worries about money, excitement when things go well, frustration at delays and problems, embarrassment at mistakes and all the rest of it. And a textbook which excludes this, no matter how invaluable the information it contains, is missing the essence of what launching your own business is all about.

As I say, it's a personal story. It will make really useful reading if you're starting – or thinking of starting – your own business. You'll find lots of subjects touched on here that I've never seen dealt with in the formal guides to starting a business. On the other hand, although I've given as much guidance as I can to all the issues we encountered along the way, you will doubtless encounter others yourself since this isn't a comprehensive guide. (You can find proper business start-up guides in any good bookshop, and I recommend you read those too.) For example, we decided to put our own money into the business, since we could start up for under £8,000. So you'll find no help here on how to raise funds. On the other hand, you'll find plenty of help on the nitty-gritty of subjects from organising phone lines or launching a PR campaign to accepting credit card payments via your website. I've explained what many of our choices were, and how we arrived at the decisions we did.

Perhaps the biggest hurdle when you start a business is making that jump from a good idea to a business which actually happens. We all have good ideas; some of those businesses I never started in the past could have been great. We all have bad ideas too, of course, and some of mine – with hindsight – were dreadful. But if you don't make that jump you'll never know. Do your research well and you'll identify the dreadful ideas before you've wasted your time and money on them. But if you never even do the research, you'll never know if you've missed the greatest humdinger of an idea you've ever had.

So how do you make that leap? Well, actually, it's not really a leap at all. It's like climbing a ladder. Just take the first step. It might be making a few phone calls or spending half a day at the library looking up industry statistics. Anything which goes beyond thinking into actually doing. You can easily step back off the rung if the idea proves to be unrealistic. If it still looks good, use that momentum to climb up one more rung, and do the next bit of work. Keep going like this, translating ideas into action and, eventually, you'll find yourself at the top of the ladder with the world at your feet.

Good luck.

2 June

Rich and I have just had a really exciting idea. Rachael Stock and Elie Ball from Pearson Education – one of our publishers – have just been down for the weekend. We were chatting about business ideas and I came up with an outline plan for a publishing business. Rich and I have talked for ages about publishing. We're both getting a bit bored with writing (wouldn't want to give it up completely, but would like something else alongside). Trouble is, there are so many publishers out there, most with a lot more money than we'd have. We didn't feel we could do it successfully without an original angle.

And then we came up with this original way of publishing. Rach and Elie seemed very enthusiastic and we think it really has potential. Very broadly, the idea is to publish non-fiction books which need a lot of individual promotion. Most publishers won't touch these books (unless they think they're going to be bestsellers) because they can't afford to promote each book individually. They like to share their marketing costs between as many titles as they can cram on the same platform.

But if we sell only these one-off titles, and aim to publish only about eight books a year, we reckon it would work. It depends on picking titles which have huge scope for promotion which we can milk fully, unlike other publishers. And the other thing we need to do is to sell them through unusual outlets – on trains, in estate agents offices, through hotels and so on. Apart from Amazon, we could avoid the bookshops entirely. The big chains charge buyers a fee just to meet them, and as a small publisher we'd never even get a meeting.

TIME ELAPSED 0 months 0 weeks 1 days

The other idea we really like is to use the business to help good causes. So we think it would be great to do one book a year, say, in collaboration with a charity. It would be a regular title but with the charity brand on it, and after paying the production costs all the profits would go to the charity.

We'd love Rach and Elie to come in with us on the project, but they already have their own irons in the fire. However, they've kindly agreed to give us all the help they can, especially with selecting titles to publish. It's going to be essential to pick the right titles – as a small publisher we couldn't afford big mistakes.

4 June

Rich and I are getting really fired up about this publishing idea. We just need to find one or two more people to do it with. We even have a name for the company – White Ladder. It came to me in a dream. It's not that I think it's an omen or anything like that, but we'd been talking and thinking about it so it was obviously playing on my mind. When I woke up I thought about it, and told Rich, and we both really liked it. It's a good strong image, it implies heading upwards (my father says you can just as well go down ladders, but I reckon everyone knows you go up ladders and down snakes). Actually, I think my brain arrived at the name as a kind of joke on the fact that I'd been watching Blackadder the night before. Black Adder / White Ladder (so snakes and ladders do come into it).

We've decided that Rich should be the MD since he's really good at the business and finance side and has plenty of experience there. I'll be Marketing Director since that's my field, so I'll deal with back-end marketing. Then we need someone to do sales and someone else to do PR, who probably both need to be in or around London.

5 June

I've put together an outline for White Ladder. It just includes the main things we've thought about so far, but it means we've got it all down before we can forget it. It also means we can show it to other people to get their input. Here it is:

WHITE LADDER PRESS

Business outline

Most publishers publish large numbers of books for relatively little profit each, except for the occasional bestseller. Very few titles reach their potential sales because the publishers cannot afford to put a big marketing drive behind every one of their many titles.

White Ladder Press will be a different kind of publishing company. The aim is to publish only a few titles (say 6 or 8 a year), and to put the maximum marketing effort behind each one. In fact, titles will be selected on their marketing potential as well as on their intrinsic quality. If they don't offer excellent PR and publicity opportunities, and lucrative sales partnerships, they won't be White Ladder books.

The key to White Ladder's success will be its ability to spot a winner and to capitalise on it.

One of the problems many small presses encounter is the near impossibility of getting their books into the major bookstores. White Ladder will avoid this drawback by using publicity and sales partnerships to sell books, rather than relying on passing trade in the bookstores. The books will be available:

- By ordering direct from White Ladder (by post, phone or fax)
- From amazon.co.uk (which can be linked via White Ladder's website)
- From any sales outlet we can partner
- Through book clubs

Once a backlist is established, White Ladder Press will also launch a mail order operation (not a book club). Most mail order book catalogues give too little information about the book; this one will give a far better idea than other catalogues of what the book is really like, including a web address to read sample text.

The list

White Ladder's titles will be selected on the basis of their potential, rather than on their subject matter, so the list will be very varied. We will avoid fiction (at least initially), and self publishing.

However, anything else goes (including republishing out of print titles). Titles must, however, fit comfortably into White Ladder's brand image. This means they will:

- Appeal to a large market
- Be quirky in some way (exactly the books mainstream publishers resist taking on because they need individualised marketing)
- Be well written and well produced

Sales and PR

The rule with sales and PR is that anything goes so long as it:
- Fits the brand
- Sells books at a profit

White Ladder will only publish books which will be featured in the national media, and which have plenty of scope for selling through non-traditional outlets. These can include supermarkets, health centres, hotel chains, banks, trains, bus stations, DIY stores, schools, corporate clients, and so on (the list is limitless). This will circumvent the usual problem of being unable to get small press books into the major bookstores.

White Ladder's approach to PR and publicity will be quirky (like the books), with memorable and entertaining events and PR stunts.

The company ethos

White Ladder Press will be strongly identified as a responsible company. Most significantly, it will publish one not-for-profit book each year in partnership with a charity (starting by year three). All profits will go to the charity. This title will fit into the regular White Ladder format of having plenty of scope for publicity and appealing to a wide market. For example, we could publish a book for The Samaritans on how to recognise if a close family member or friend is suicidal, and what to do about it.

The charities White Ladder works with will be:
- UK based
- People oriented
- Non-political and non-controversial

White Ladder will be a flexible and family-friendly company, allowing its members to telework, and to fit work around family commitments. It will pay all suppliers promptly, especially freelances and small businesses, and will be co-operative and easy to do business with.

White Ladder's approach to business will be fun. We will only publish books we enjoy and believe in, and we will have a quirky and interesting approach to PR, publicity and sales. We want to stay small and sleep nights.

Company structure

White Ladder will be a small business, which will aim to stay small. Rather than produce more than about ten books a year, we will aim to grow by:
- Publishing highly profitable titles
- Marketing a successful backlist

White Ladder will have three or four full-time (or roughly full-time) executive directors, each with a 25% share:
- MD
- Marketing director – dealing with back-end marketing from product development and print buying to promotional materials and mail order.
- PR director – responsible for achieving maximum publicity for each title, placing features and ads, and getting full media coverage. Probably London-based.
- Sales director – arranging partnership deals and finding original and lucrative outlets for the books. Also setting up the charity books. Probably London-based.
(PR and sales may be one combined job.)

In time, when the money grows, White Ladder will take on two to three additional staff as PAs/administrative assistants. We don't anticipate growing beyond this size. Functions such as order fulfilment will be outplaced.

Selecting titles

White Ladder will use an editorial board of experienced and talented people to select titles for publication. These people will be essential to the success of the venture. This editorial board will meet every two to three months to discuss and agree which titles have enough potential to be worth publishing. All the executive directors will be part of the board, along with two or three other people of judgement and publishing experience.

Having written the outline I've emailed it to Rach and Elie, Mark Hayward (our agent), and Tony (my father). Let's wait and see if they think it has any potential.

GOLDEN RULE: *Get your ideas down on paper. That way you can see them clearly. And you can always adapt them later; indeed you almost certainly will.*

6 June

Had a reply from Mark very promptly (as always). He seems to be broadly encouraging, although he came up with a few reservations (which is much more helpful than just telling us what we've got right). I think they're all useful points and none of them is an insurmountable obstacle. Here's the email:

Roni

Thanks for sending this over. It's intriguing.

I certainly agree with the central proposition that most publishers overpublish and underpromote. Although I can understand the rationale for doing so. Publishing is based on a number of rules of thumb. One (unspoken, obviously) is that you never know what will sell and what won't, so you're better off publishing 10 books haphazardly in the hope that one will hit the big time rather than publishing one with 100% commitment only to find that it dies a death.

Anyway, to play the devil's advocate...

The success of the venture (given that you can produce a quality product, upon which all else depends) relies on two things: publicity and distribution. You have to let people know the books exist. And you have to make them available to the public. There are ways and means for small publishers to punch above their weight in terms of publicity, which you've rightly identified. The advent of e-commerce, viral marketing, the Internet, etc. also opens up lots of avenues for marketing and advertising which are relatively cheap.

I see the central problem being distribution. I'm not convinced that you could generate enough volume in direct sales and Internet sales to create the sort of bestsellers that you are looking for. Even having a few weeks of really good publicity and media coverage will only generate off the page sales as long as the books are in the spotlight. And to be a featured book on Amazon or in a bookshop window (corrupt, cruel world that we live in) costs a lot of money. Rachael could tell you how much, but it'd be a lot for a small publisher.

For the sort of bestseller volumes that I think you are looking for you need to be in Smiths and in the supermarkets and non-traditional outlets. Bookshops are useful too but (depending on the type of books you will be publishing) actually not as crucial as you might imagine – really explosive volume sales come in the high-discount, high-volume outlets.

[Case in point – a client who had her novel published a month or so ago sold 10,000 copies in Asda in the first month, 5,000 in Woolworths and Smiths have just come in with an order for 3,000. She went to ask a friendly bookseller in her local Waterstones if they'd had the book. She checked on the computer and told her that Waterstones had sold the grand total of 11 copies of her book. Nationwide.]

Now even the biggest publishers struggle to get in Smiths. Even Hodder Headline struggle and they're part of Smiths. So I'm not sure there's an easy answer. But it seems to me that you have to look to get in someone who has a solid track record of getting books into book clubs, Smiths, supermarkets, the non-traditional outlets, etc. That's my hunch, anyway.

The bookshop sales will (I guess?) be handled through one of the independent distributors. But then you'll be one small publisher on a list of 50 that the reps sell into the shops in a very desultory and half-hearted way (that was my experience as a bookseller anyway), which means that you also have to raise your profile amongst booksellers so that they will know where to find you to order books direct. Good relationships with the trade press are crucial. Get the books into the quarterly round-ups of forthcoming titles – targeted free advertising. An old friend of mine is an editorial manager at The Bookseller, responsible for putting these together, which could be useful...

Incidentally, if you are interested in exploring some of the possibilities of promoting and selling on the web I'd be happy to put you in touch with Bob Cotton who's another client. Funnily enough, Bob's writing a book for Capstone right now on E-Selling so he's thinking about all these sort of things at the moment, and he's something of a guru on web design and everything "e-business". I'm sure he'd be willing to give you some input and if you're looking to commission someone to build a web presence then, if he's not the right man to do it, I bet he can recommend someone top notch.

A couple of other things I'd throw into the melting pot:

How about expanding the idea of partnership beyond one book for charity each year? Branded books are a great way to link your product up to something people feel familiar and comfortable with.

And what are your plans for subsidiary rights? Obviously with the sort of popular non-fiction you're talking about serial sales are crucial. But what about TV, film, translation, audio, US, etc... I'd think about employing sub-agents (and this is something we would be happy to consider if you are interested) to handle these rights on your behalf. I've recently started representing The Collins Press, a small publisher in Ireland, to sell on UK and US rights as well as TV/Film rights in the cream of their list. An arrangement like that can be a useful extra revenue stream.

Do you have precedents in mind for the sort of publishing operation you would want to set up? There are some good, small independents in the UK but they tend to be single niche, lower volume operations like Codex (SF) or No Exit (Crime), catering to a limited, dedicated readership, which makes marketing a hell of a lot easier. There is an odd outfit in the States called McSweeneys, which is a journal, a bookshop, a website and a small publishing house combined. The website is worth a look anyway – www.mcsweeneys.net – if only for their agony uncle column "Ask a Former Professional Literary Agent". They also have the funniest and most honest submission guidelines in publishing.

Anyhow, hope some of this is useful.

All best,
Mark

Actually, this is really useful. We reckon Mark's right about needing to be in bookshops – or at least needing to be accessible to bookshops so that if we generate enough publicity the bookshops can order the books easily. And he's right that good promotion can get you a lot of initial sales, but how do you keep selling when the publicity dies down? We need to think of plenty of outlets for long term sales.

We've checked out mcsweeney's and he's right – their submission guidelines are wonderful.

For some bizarre reason, Rich came up with an idea for business cards (I'm sure we don't need to think about this for months, but it all helps get us clearly focused so we followed it through). He suggested a folded and die-cut card that stands up like a white ladder, or a set of library steps. I did a mock up, with his name and job title on the inside card showing through the cutout steps. Actually, Rich and I are keen not to get too serious, and reading the mcsweeney's stuff made us realise that you don't have to be. Rich loved the business card, but hated being called 'Managing Director' – much too formal and pompous and grown up. So we've changed our job titles. Rich is 'The Big Cheese' and I'm 'Brains' (you can tell the kids are into Thunderbirds at the moment).

I also found myself doodling with logo designs. Maybe the 'H' of 'white' could be a ladder, with perhaps a stylised jester climbing up it.

> **GOLDEN RULE:** *Don't just think about it – do something. Talk to people, check out some facts and figures. This activity is what gives you the momentum to turn your idea from a pipe-dream into a reality.*

7 June

I've talked to Tony, my father, who is really useful on lots of things, especially setting up a business. He has lots of info about how they started Video Arts. Apparently he had more money to put in than the others, but he wanted all the directors to have an equal share. Otherwise if there was a choice between bigger dividends or raises in salary, the board would be split according to what size share everyone had. So they gave everyone an equal share. Instead of putting his money into the company, he notionally put it into the first film. He took the biggest royalty from that film to pay back his investment, leaving everyone with an equal stake in the business itself.

He recommended issuing lots of shares, say 10,000, so that they can easily be given or sold later in small quantities. He says if you have only 100 shares it's surprising how fast they can disappear if you decide to give one here and a couple there.

Tony also advised not to give away more equity than we need to. This touches on a sticky issue for me and Rich. We reckon we need two more directors, but we're not sure we agree about whether to pay them a salary or whether to sell them a share (or share options). I'm worried that someone with no stake in the business could just leave any time with a month's notice. If they did this just before the launch of a new title we could be in big trouble. However, if they have a stake they'll want to see a good replacement in post before they go. As Tony points out, this only works if they've invested enough in the business that it hurts to walk away (so share options wouldn't really help).

One of the problems with paying a salary is that we haven't got any money. Quite a big problem really. There's always commission, but I don't think you get the best people on commission only. It may be a new and exciting idea, but if it's not their idea, why should they invest all that time for nothing with no guaranteed return? People have tried to get me to do this in the past, and I've always been very wary. I always think, "If you're so sure you've got such a great idea, put your money where your mouth is and pay me an honest wage for the work you want out of me."

Still, as Rich feels more strongly than I do, we don't want to give away more equity than we need. So the jury's still out on this one.

10 June

Spoke to Rach today, who was full of useful information. She loves the outline, and thinks the idea has great potential. She gave me all sorts of useful facts and figures, although they are based on large publishers' costs. In some cases – such as discounts – these are very similar, but costs need to be treated as very rough guides only. Here are my notes on the phone call:

WHITE LADDER – costings info

Discounts

Wholesalers	30%
Waterstones	40-45%
WHSmiths	50%
Overseas distributors	70%
Affiliate partners (w link to our website)	15%
Bookclubs	60-70%
amazon.co.uk	35-45%
Amazon with price promo	50+% (but worth the extra)
Corporates	up tp 70% for (5-10,000+ copies)

- Smaller corporate deals operate on a unit price; reckon to make 4-5 times the unit cost (excluding overheads)
- Link via website to Amazon, i.e. amazon.co.uk affiliate partner, and get 10-15% commission on sales
- Wholesalers are worth considering (e.g. Bertrams, Gardners) as they sell to independents. They are often the first stop for bookshops and Amazon when looking for a supplier.

Quantities

Suppose b&w, paperback, 100-150pp:

- Generally uneconomic to print less than 3,000 initial run, and 1,000 for reprints
- Paper, print and bind (ppb) about 50-60p per unit
- Unit cost – ppb plus proof, copyedit, design and setting – about £1.20-1.30 per unit
- If book length drops ppb costs will reduce in rough proportion, but proof, edit, design and setting costs will reduce by less

Above figures include Pearson Ed's bulk discounts on ppb so allow a little more

Printing

Black&white – cheapest in UK

Colour – Europe, usually Italy/Spain. SE Asia is cheaper, but shipping etc makes it less practical

Digital printing – can print efficiently in much smaller quantities but the quality is still not as good as traditional printing methods

Overall costings

Suppose b&w, retailing at £5-10:

- Say average 40% discount
- 10,000 copies sold is generally minimum to make it worthwhile
- 15,000 over 2 years (10 in first year, 5 in second) is good
- 20-30,000 is possible if title is right and PR/selling is good
- Reckon to sell at reasonable levels for 3-4 years

Rach came up with lots of other useful comments, most notably the fact that she's certain that sales and PR could both be handled by one person, at least to begin with. This is encouraging, especially since we can't even find one other person yet (although there's plenty of time). Then again, Rich and I wonder how easy it would be for a third person to work alongside the two of us. As Rich says, we have meetings in the bath, in bed at 2 o'clock in the morning, over break-fast – it could be very difficult for a third person to feel included, especially if they need to be based four hours away in London.

We've been saying we wouldn't publish our own books, because we don't want to look like a vanity publisher and we're not sure our judgement is as reliable for our own books as for other people's. But I asked Rachael about this, and she didn't think it was a problem. If we were worried, she pointed out, we could always write under another name.

One of the reasons for this is that we think my book *Family Matters*, about applying business techniques to bringing up children (negoti-ating skills, team building etc) would be good. It's out in the US and selling very well apparently, but we can't seem to sell the UK rights. Publishers keep saying, 'lovely idea but it doesn't fit in with the rest of our parenting list – it's a bit wacky'. Well, that's exactly what White Ladder is supposed to be about. The other title we like is one of Rich's called *The Voice of Tobacco*. It's a give up smoking book with a difference – again a bit quirky for most publishers. Rachael likes both ideas, and would be inclined to start with *Family Matters* because it has more obvious sales channels to exploit.

12 June

I've had an idea I really like for selling books. London black cabs. If we can persuade cabbies to sell books for us, they could sell to a captive audience and keep the mark-up themselves. Everyone benefits. You'd need the right book – maybe Voice of Tobacco. Half of them would hate it but half would love it, and you need the kind of book the cabbies would have a strong affinity with.

20 June

Spoke to Mark Allin at Capstone – extremely useful. He reckons the two areas we really need to focus on are the brand itself, and the back end processes. His input is incredibly useful since he and Richard started Capstone themselves. Here are my notes on the conversation:

WHITE LADDER

Comments from Mark Allin

Generally very positive. Good idea, especially being marketing-driven and going for unusual outlets.

2 main areas that need more work: brand focus, and back end processes

Focus

Any new publisher needs a story, an explanation of what

gap in the market they can fill and how. It may change over time, but it needs to be clear, focused and explainable at the outset. It could be to do with content, price, format. It might be, for example, lifeskills with a twist. Develop a strapline – 'independent living, independent thinking', 'outside the mainstream', that sort of thing.

Distribution

- Selling through big book chains is optional. If we do, ideally it should be via a sales consortium or a publisher. Could mail booksellers direct but just because they like the idea it doesn't mean they'll buy the books. Might be safer to use an intermediary. Could talk to Simon, Capstone's ex-Sales Director.
- Worth joining the Independent Publisher's Guild (IPG) and asking for their lists of sales reps, distributors etc. Ask Mark to let us know the pros and cons of each.
- Book clubs might be worthwhile if selling through a rep or publisher.
- Need to be in with the big 3 wholesalers. Amazon, for example, wouldn't deal direct but only through wholesalers. Price promos with Amazon are generally worth doing.
- Good idea to use a distributor to handle warehousing, fulfilment, invoicing etc. They collect the money and settle up at the end of each month. They generally charge between 8-15%. They must be reliable and have a good reputation or wholesalers, retailers and online outlets won't deal with them.

General

- Capstone plan titles 9 months ahead. Any shorter isn't really feasible because outlets and wholesalers need advance planning time.

- Think about doing deals with big organisations who will take 75% and upwards of the books. Original approaches to sponsorship etc are a good prospect for earning. Could do one or two titles a year of this kind.
- Capstone – just Mark and Richard for first year, then a secretary too, then a sales director in third year. Now 6 people and £3.6m turnover (as part of Wiley).
- Talk to accountant re putting royalties through the company rather than paying them direct.

Probably the most useful thing of all to come out of this in the short term was that Mark and Richard were on their own to begin with, and didn't take on any help with sales until the third year. Rich and I seem to have moved towards the view that we don't need anyone else initially and can launch White Ladder on our own.

This also sidesteps all debates about who to use or how to pay them.

Mark has offered to come down to Devon for a day in August to talk to us, and to show us their initial sales forecasts and so on. Incredibly helpful.

GOLDEN RULE: *Talk to everyone you can.* This is one big reason why it's an enormous help to start a business in an industry you already know about. But even if you have no contacts at all, you'll still find helpful people if you ask around.

24 June

Rich has a terrific idea for a sales outlet – pubs. We'd love to see 'Voice of Tobacco' in counter packs on the bar. We'd need to talk to brewery chains about it. Digital printing means we could print a few copies only and test them in local pubs to see how they go. If they do well it will help us in dealing with big pub chains.

30 June

I've been talking to a friend of mine, Peter, recently about a business he started with three other people. Three of the four of them had clearly put in a huge amount of work, but what was the fourth one there for? Peter said that actually it had been a mistake inviting Keith to join them. Not Keith's fault at all, but actually they just didn't need him. The same went for Mike, who joined them later. They thought the business would go in certain directions which it didn't, making both Keith and Mike unnecessary really. When they finally sold the business, there was some resentment that Keith and Mike made as much out of it as the others.

It reinforces Rich's and my view that we should do everything ourselves until we're certain we need someone else, and then think twice about giving them a significant share.

We've been talking for about a month now about White Ladder, and we're really fired up about it. I'm ridiculously nervous about it – I think I feel a bit swamped by the idea of all those technical bits like registering it and stuff. Fortunately, however, Rich is on top of all that and has sorted it all out. We've registered the company as White Ladder Press Limited. We think it's essential we limit the company since we don't want to lose everything we have, even though being limited gives us more onerous accounting requirements. Being a married couple as well as business partners, if we were to incur debts we'd both be in trouble and that's the whole family in the shit.

REGISTERING THE COMPANY

You can register a new company through Companies House, or via websites such as **www.companyformations.ltd.uk** or **www.uk-plc.net/companyformation/**. Or you can look at the ads in Exchange and Mart. The websites will tell you the rules about what names you can and can't have (not an existing company name, for example, or words like 'royal').

To register as a limited company you must have at least one director plus a company secretary (who can also be a director if you wish).

Cost: £42.50 + VAT if you buy a name off the shelf (in other words, you choose from a list of preselected names). If you choose your own name, as we have, it costs £55 + VAT.

LIMITED COMPANY OR NOT?

There are three main ways you can set up your company, each with their own pros and cons: sole trader, partnership or limited company.

Sole trader

This means doing business under your own name, with no requirement to keep specific records unless you register for VAT (although the tax man will need you to declare your income and produce paperwork to back it up).

Not being a limited company you are personally liable for your business's debts, so in theory you can lose your house and/or other possessions if the business goes under owing money. You also can't sell equity to raise extra capital for the business.

On the plus side, this is the simplest and cheapest operation to run, you can start trading tomorrow, and you don't have to file financial information or have your accounts audited. You'll pay Schedule D tax, in other words you declare your earnings at the end of the year and pay tax on them rather than earning PAYE.

Partnership

If you agree to run your business with someone else (or several someone elses) with the intention of sharing the profits, you will probably be recognised as a partnership by law even if you didn't realise it yourself.

Partnerships share many of the advantages of being a sole trader. However, the most significant point to consider is that each partner is liable for their own and their partner's trading debts. So if your partner goes bankrupt or does a runner, you become solely responsible for the entire debt (unless you are registered as a limited, or sleeping, partner). For this reason, partners are strongly recommended to draw up a partnership contract covering such issues as:

- profit sharing
- responsibilities
- decision-making powers
- valuing and realising capital
- taking time off for illness, holidays, maternity leave etc
- accountancy procedures

If you are a couple going into business together, you should certainly draw up such a contract if there is the slightest possibility that the relationship might ever split up.

A partnership can give you some access to additional equity since a sleeping partner can put money into the business.

Limited company

The big thing here is that the business has its own identity separate from its owners, which means that any debts it incurs cannot be claimed from the directors (unless they have been trading illegally or incompetently in some way). To form a limited company you must have at least two shareholders, at least one of whom must be a director.

The big advantages here are the fact that your personal liability is limited (a big plus in our case) and the ability to raise capital by selling shares. There's also a plus in the fact that it makes you sound like a professional business and has a higher status image than a partnership or sole trader.

On the minus side, directors must be paid PAYE, and if your

turnover is over a certain level you have to have some kind of audit. Also, you have to have a certificate of incorporation before you can start trading, and there is more expense involved in registering, accounting and so on than if you simply set up as a sole trader or partnership.

2 July

We've decided that if we want a website (which we do) we should register a domain name as soon as we can, before it goes. Is whiteladder available? Rich (again) has checked this out, and has registered whiteladder.com, whiteladderpress.com and whiteladderpress.co.uk. The one we couldn't get is whiteladder.co.uk. We decided to register all three because we don't know yet which we want to use – that way we keep our options open. In any case we'll probably keep the others and use them as forwarding sites.

REGISTERING THE DOMAIN NAMES

You can do this via websites such as **www.register.com** (which is the one we used). Or search under, for example, domain +register. These sites invite you to key in the domain name you want to use, and they then tell you whether it's available. It will often be available with certain suffixes only. For example, we could get whiteladder.com but not whiteladder.co.uk.

Cost: It depends on the suffix you choose, up to a point. For example, .com, .net and .org all cost $70 for two years (with the option of registering for one, five or ten years). It's a little cheaper, $63 for two years, if you opt for .info or .biz. If you want a .co.uk suffix, it's $90 for two years.

I've got to get the book I'm writing out of the way by the middle of July. We're going to keep talking until then, and once it's delivered I'll concentrate on putting together a business plan.

15 July

Time for the business plan. I can hardly think where to start, but I've got a good book on business plans (I ought to know all this anyway, but my mind's gone blank when it comes to our own plan). Using the book, although with a few adaptations of my own, I've prepared a 20-odd page business plan. It needs some fleshing out still. Well, actually, almost all the pages are completely blank with just a heading at the top. But it tells us what we need to find out and then we can just fill in the blanks. The pages are:

1 Cover page
2 Mission statement
3 Business outline
4 Company ethos
5 Key people
6 The titles
7 The customers
8 The competition
9 White Ladder online

10 SWOT analysis

11 Objectives

12 Sales forecast

13 Marketing strategy

14 Profit and loss forecast

15 Cash flow forecast

16 Capital expenditure

17 Financial base

18 Management information systems

I've updated and copied across the business outline, company ethos and key people stuff, and we'd got about halfway through the mission statement so I put that in too even though it wasn't complete. Most of the stuff about the titles was written, and I added a bit about how many titles per year. I also filled in the pages about

- White Ladder online
- Capital expenditure (that was easy – just one line: 'We don't anticipate any significant capital expenditure in the first two years')
- Financial base (easy again – we'll put in our own money)

That only leaves about nine sections. The nine longest sections. Still, I've got plenty of time at the moment. The aim is to complete the business plan by the end of the summer. That gives me about 6 weeks. There'll be odd bits still to add no doubt, and it will be constantly tweaked, but we should have something useful and showable by then.

Actually, it's already proving useful. Rich and I were talking about it last night and it drew our attention to all sorts of things we hadn't considered fully before. We were trying to finalise the mission statement, and thinking about it so hard raised lots of interesting questions. We realised that we needed to be very clear about what does and doesn't constitute a White Ladder book. Are they always teach-ing something? Are they always quirky? Always humorous? These are all qualities we'd been thinking of as White Ladder ones, but we needed to decide whether we wanted them to be compulsory.

We decided that we want all our titles to be offbeat in some way, but not necessarily humorous. We also want them all to teach in the sense of imparting useful, functional information. They don't need to be instructional in style, however, and we don't want to use the word 'teach' to imply that they are 'how-to' books.

It was Mark Allin who first recommended that we go through the process of writing a mission statement or at least a strapline early in the process. Quite right too – it's been an invaluable exercise. We decided on the strapline 'new tricks for old dogs' (subject to testing it out on a few people once the business plan is ready to show round). We like it because:

- It indicates that White Ladder books are about taking traditional subjects and looking at them from a new or offbeat angle
- It's a more catchy and memorable image than the usual boring abstract straplines (along the lines of 'taking a new angle' or 'creativity with style' kind of crap)
- We think the image has a touch of humour – we could even incor-porate it in some way into our logo

I was slightly concerned that it might appear that we were calling our readers old dogs. But we both decided that we didn't care. Most read-ers don't even notice who's published the book they're reading, let alone what their slogan is. Although we'd like to build up a mail order list of direct customers who *do* know who we are. But more to the point, we think our kind of readers will have the sense of humour to realise the strapline is tongue in cheek if they do happen to notice it.

TIME ELAPSED   1 months   2 weeks   1 days

MISSION STATEMENT

The mission statement needs to talk about the *company's* mission, not ours. So it's not 'to publish books and make lots of money'. It's about the company's raison d'être. Even the books are only a means to an end, so we want to talk about the end purpose itself. We looked at a couple of other organisations' mission statements to help us:

3M: To solve unsolved problems innovatively
Wal-Mart: To give ordinary folk the chance to buy the same thing as rich people
Disney: To make people happy

These are often backed up by four or five one-liner statements of values – we incorporated these into the mission statement itself. So our mission statement now reads:

We want to teach old dogs new tricks. We want to intrigue, entertain and be useful at the same time. And we want to use our mainstream business to benefit good causes, so we'll do that too. We'll have fun or there's no point being in business, and we'll give fun to everyone else around us – our customers, our partners, our suppliers... even our postman.

GOLDEN RULE: *Write your mission statement.* Do this early on because it will help you focus your mind on what exactly your new business is there for.

18 July

Doing the SWOT analysis together last night after supper was a really useful exercise. We considered our strengths and weaknesses and it got us thinking about various things, from who our editorial advisors should be (a good pool of advisors is one of our strengths) to the fact that we need to work out how to forecast for returns (books are always sold on a sale or return basis). We'll be particularly vulnerable to returns, being small, so that was one of our weaknesses.

We may also need to plan a long way ahead if we want to sell first serial rights etc, which is a weakness to set against the typical small business strength of being able to move much faster than the big, lumbering established competitors.

SWOT ANALYSIS

This simply stands for:

- Strengths
- Weaknesses
- Opportunities
- Threats

It's a list of the plusses and minuses of the business – not what we'd like them to be but what they really are. Strengths and weaknesses are internal factors about the business itself: low overheads, highly motivated staff, that sort of thing are strengths; and as weaknesses, stuff like poor location (being in Devon), limited funds and so on.

Opportunities and threats come from outside the business –

things such as gaps in the market, competitors going bust, and so on. One of our opportunities, for example, is the advent of digital printing technology, which means we'll soon be able to print single copies of a book to order, rather than having to run off a few thousand copies at a time.

GOLDEN RULE: *Write a business plan.* Even if you don't need to raise any funds and no one but you will ever see it, this process is invaluable for drawing your attention to all sorts of issues you need to think about. Over 90% of businesses that fail had no business plan.

19 July

Spoke to Mark Hayward about selling serial rights. He reckons we've got time to sell serial rights for the first book if we publish in April, assuming we're ready to commit ourselves to the book – and White Ladder – by about September. That way we could publish *Voice of Tobacco* in September/October next year and catch the New Year (resolutions) market.

Mark thinks we could get between about £2-5,000 for serial rights, probably half payable up front, which would be a big help with funding the first book.

Rich and I have been talking about promotion and PR. We reckon that with limited funds we concentrate on promoting the book. Once it's selling, and there's some money to spend, then we can worry about promoting the White Ladder brand. Essentially we need to promote the brand to booksellers and the book to readers.

23 July

We've been working more on the business plan, although we haven't yet reached the stage where we can put figures together. We're also reading every book we can lay our hands on about publishing, publishing online, marketing for publishers and whatever else we can think of.

Today I had an incredibly useful conversation with Susan Hill (the novelist, who also has her own small publishing company), who is a good friend of my parents. She was enormously helpful and talked to me for ages with masses of useful tips and information.

Unlike Mark Allin at Capstone, Susan does everything herself – order taking, packing up books, distribution and so on. Interestingly, she is also the only publisher I've spoken to who has no problem with returns. Returns are the bane of most publishers' lives: books are supplied on sale or return and the more that are returned, the more complicated (and depressing) the accounting becomes, as well as the time and hassle of processing the returns physically. Susan reckons that returns are the result of overselling – if you persuade bookshops to take more books than they can sell, you're bound to get returns. If you don't pressure the bookshops, all you need to do is generate interest in the book and the shops will come to you anyway.

Rich and I talked at length about Susan's way of doing things, and we much prefer the hands-on approach she adopts. My concern had

TIME ELAPSED 1 months 3 weeks 2 days

been that if you did your own order fulfilment and accounting, you'd have no time left actually to sell the damn things. But this isn't Susan's experience. She points out that it's far cheaper to employ a few local teenagers for a couple of weekends to clear a rush of orders, than to pay a distributor a percentage of every book you sell. In fact, you don't have to be turning over that much stock before a permanent employee could do the job cheaper than a distributor.

And what's more, you are in control of your business. If a customer calls and says their order hasn't arrived, you know how to chase it up because you despatched the order yourself.

So all in all, we think we'll go for the DIY approach. We reckon we'll have more fun and save money too. However, I'd like to run it past a few other people first.

Another useful thing to come out of the conversation was the advice that it's worth having your own website, with ordering facilities, from the start. It costs relatively little to set up and maintain. This is encouraging, as we didn't really want the only online ordering option to be via Amazon, simply because of the discount they take. The more books you can sell direct, the more money you can make, since average discounts to booksellers are about 40%.

Susan had all sorts of helpful comments and contacts to put us in touch with; here's a copy of the notes I made on our conversation.

WHITE LADDER
Notes from Susan Hill

Long Barn Books
- Started 6 years ago with own book, then *How to Beat Sir Humphrey*, then four more in first year

- Policy now is to publish fewer books which sell well – now publishes only about 4 a year – no time for more (given all her other commitments)
- Currently 2 in print, 2 in print but not for much longer, 1 coming out next year (so far)
- Never lost money on a book, made more money each year than the year before
- Pre-tax profit was over £10,000 in first year; last year (to April) was £50,000
- Duchess of Devonshire's book launched last Xmas, has now sold 43,000. Expecting to sell another 20,000 with imminent newspaper deal
- LBB will publish anything they think will sell – no need to stick to a niche
- Never publish to tie in with a passing fad, such as eclipse or jubilee – you can get left with a lot of useless stock

White Ladder
- General idea excellent
- In our case, fine to self publish and makes good sense
- The word 'Press' has overtones of 'weaving your own garments' – slightly 'arty amateurish'
- Non-booksellers don't like selling books – and want unviable deals – doesn't think pubs would go for *Voice of Tobacco*, better to sell into doctors' surgeries etc – 'book is cheaper than the cost of a prescription' (but make it easy for them to process orders – they're not set up to sell over the counter)
- Mail order very good idea, especially with 'join our club for free' offer – including special discount/free book/bogof ('buy one get one free') etc

Printing

- Great skill is in knowing how many to print – better too few than too many.
- The Bath Press (Susan's printers) now own 60% of printers in UK; Clays of Bungay own about 36%
- For a first run of a paperback allow 3 weeks at the printers (more in August/September)
- Don't economise on paper. Quality pays. Upgrading the paper from average to good will cost maybe half a penny per book, and it's well worth it. People notice and comment.
- Printers should overprint at least about 50 covers for publicity use
- For page design talk to Julie Martin on 01732 885212 (she's in Sevenoaks). Brilliant page designer, and she can probably recommend jacket designers

Distribution

- Do it yourself: it's cheaper to take on short term packers occasionally than to pay a distributor a permanent percentage
- Susan will, e.g., employ 6 local teenagers for a weekend if there's a rush on
- Then mail out or send by carrier
- The business is 'feast or famine' – mad rush or nothing to do
- Need good contacts at Bertrams and Gardners (Susan will introduce us)
- Store your own books, but remember that paper absorbs damp and keep the heat on low even in summer, or you'll lose all your stock
- Do your own packing and despatch – buy bulk supplies of packing materials when they're on offer. Susan never pays full price for anything.

- Deliver by return of post, and generally give good service
- Don't wait for cheques to clear – 'people who buy books are always honest' – Susan's never had a bad cheque in 6 years
- Always offer free p&p. It's worth it, and still far cheaper than using a distributor

Accounting etc

- Should get free business banking for first 2 years for a new business (she's with HSBC)
- Try to get paid by anything other than cheque (e.g. BACS) to avoid extra charges
- Susan has no bad debtors, though most bookshops pay on 90 days but you must follow their payment system if you want them to pay you on time. She's never had to remind Waterstones, but the independents often need a polite memory jog
- Susan accepts credit cards, but discourages phone bookings (because she doesn't have a dedicated business line and hates taking orders at 9 o'clock in the evening)
- Remember to register with the data protection registrar if doing mail order/keeping people's details

Publication

- Only launch in time for Xmas if you really have to – there's too much competition in shops and for features in the media
- Avoid most of July, and August
- Aim to launch January to June, or September. Maybe beginning of October
- Stagger publications dates so you can focus on one book at a time, and there's less rush for order fulfilment

Promotion

- Just promote the titles, don't worry about promoting the brand
- 20 review copies is generally plenty – just target them well
- Use extra covers from printer
- Use local radio, regional newspapers etc, especially with a '3 free books to first people to phone' kind of promotion
- Also go for Woman's Hour (parenting), Midweek (tobacco)
- Print a leaflet/flyer for each book, using artwork from cover (4-colour etc). Either A5 or A6, always with order form on the back.
- Print about 10,000 leaflets – use RCS (they have a goldfish logo) who advertise in Exchange & Mart – really cheap and well worth it. Leave them around/send them out anywhere you can
- 'Never send a book out without a leaflet for another book in it'

Website

- Have it ready to go about when 1st title is launched, but don't panic to the day
- Well worth doing – even with cost of netbanx etc it's still cheaper than selling via bookshops
- Susan sells roughly 20 books a week – across her list – via her website
- Check out: **www.susan-hill.com**, **www.booksandcompany.co.uk**, and **www.thewomaninblack.com**.
  Booksand company is her magazine, which includes Long Barn Books website.
- Contact her website people who are cheap and excellent,

and design and maintain for whatever budget you give them: Guy Courtenay (and Tom), Pedalo Ltd: guy@pedalo.co.uk

Bookshops

- Just need to know the right people at Waterstones and Smiths – Susan can introduce us
- So long as you only offer books which are suitable and already have good publicity, they'll be interested
- If the book generates enough publicity, they'll come to you
- In general, 'always get people to come to you, because then you can dictate the terms'
- Waterstones approached Susan to ask for 6,000 specially printed paperback copies of the Duchess of Devonshire's book (it was only available in h/b)
- Independents – get publicity first, especially features in national press. Then generate a press release highlighting the feature (s). Then spend a boring couple of hours faxing it round all the independents – 'independent bookshops take notice of faxes'
- Book clubs – don't approach them, wait for them to come to you. Not always worth it (she's been approached once and ended up turning it down), but can be. She doesn't think the publicity is much use to her; the image is a bit cheap.

Returns

- Almost no returns – maybe 20 on Duchess of Devonshire's book (out of 43,000), all because of damage or printing error.
- Don't oversell to bookshops. "You haven't sold 500 copies to Waterstone's, you're storing 500 copies in their stores instead of in your own warehouse, and they'll all come back eventually."

TIME ELAPSED

■ Find out what will sell first, then only get shops to stock in the right numbers.

24 July

It's time we sorted out costings in a bit more detail. And we're starting to get somewhere. I spoke to Susan's page designer today – Julie – whose prices seem very reasonable. If we give her a manuscript on disk, she can turn it into a book, essentially, and then send the disk direct to the printers. In between these two ends of the process we get to look at proofs and so on so we can make sure we get what we want. She can design book jackets for us too.

Meanwhile, Rich has been talking to Susan's recommended website designers, and is getting a quote from them.

31 July

I spoke to our local printer today about printing stationery – we just want prices at this stage so we can work out costings. We'll manage on letterheads, comp slips and business cards to begin with. It looks as if it will cost around £100 to design a logo, and the rest of the printing will be around £400 (that's because we want fancy business cards, die cut in the shape of a ladder).

Rich and I had a lengthy debate about whether or not we hold with supplying bookshops sale or return. Rich disapproves thoroughly and said we simply shouldn't do it. If bookshops won't buy outright we just won't supply them. I argued that since it's standard practice throughout the industry there was probably a reason for it, and to refuse to do it could mean we go out of business. Eventually we decided to compromise – after talking to other people in the industry about it. The compromise we thought of was that we restrict the number or percentage of returns we allow per bookshop. So they can order as many copies as they like, but we won't accept more than two of them back, or more than twenty percent back, or whatever figure we decide.

What was interesting about the whole discussion was that it highlighted our different approaches. Rich is all for making policy on the basis of some broad, sweeping principle without researching it first, while I think we should check things out very thoroughly before we differ from the norm. While my approach is more sober and careful, without Rich we'd never have questioned the practice and arrived at a successful compromise at all.

I've been reading a book called *The Beermat Entrepreneur* which is all about starting a business. It describes the personality of the entrepreneur – charismatic and sometimes hot-headed among other traits – and says that a good entrepreneur needs to be supported by what the author calls 'cornerstones' who are less of a driving force, but who keep the entrepreneur in check. Well, Rich is definitely the entrepreneur, and I'm the cornerstone.

> I can thoroughly recommend The Beermat Entrepreneur, by Mike Southon and Chris West, published by Prentice Hall. It seems primarily aimed at slightly larger start-up operations than ours, but it still has some useful stuff in it for us.

TIME ELAPSED **1** months **4** weeks **3** days

1 August

After yesterday's discussion we decided we should talk to local book-shop managers/owners about how they decide what to order, in what quantities and so on. In fact, of course, regardless of yesterday's conversation we should do this. Rich phoned round and talked to our local independent bookshop manager, who told him that the big wholesalers set the sale or returns policy, and not the publishers. So much for our discussion then; we don't get much say in it. However, we would hope also to supply bookshops direct – it saves us the wholesalers' discount – so we can still adopt a limited sale or return policy when we supply direct. We're meeting the manager of our local branch of Ottakers next week.

7 August

I've been looking at the costs of setting up White Ladder – we can't complete our business plan until we can put together a cash flow forecast and a profit and loss. Our costs divide in two essentially: the cost of publishing the first book, and the cost of setting up the business. Our list of expenses looks like this:

Costs per title
Advance, if any (that's the downpayment to the author)
Royalties
Page layouts
Jacket design

Printing and delivery
Leaflets (design)
Leaflets (print)

General start-up costs
Logo design
Website
Stationery
Contracts advice
Post and packing
General office costs (receipts, invoices, paper etc)

We now have to get figures for all of these. They can't be precise since some things are charged by the hour or day, such as website design, so you don't get an exact figure until the job is completed. And we don't have exact specifications for things like cover designs yet. But we're getting as accurate quotes as we can, and we're over rather than under estimating so if there are any surprises, they'll be pleasant ones.

We won't have to pay an advance on our first couple of titles since they'll be our own, so that will save us a couple of thousand at least.

We've talked to website designers and we seem to have to pay for:

- Website design
- Registering with search engines
- Setting up the e-commerce facility (we want customers to be able to order direct from the website)
- Website hosting
- Updating the site (that's an ongoing and not an initial cost, of course)

. looks as though we can do all this very professionally and slickly for inside about £1,500.

We've talked about what we want from the website and we want it to be:

- Very professional (not an off-the-peg type design)
- Clean and simple
- Fast to download
- As few pages as possible
- Equipped with a counter so we know how many hits we get (but we don't want this visible to the customer)

As far as the pages themselves are concerned, we're looking at:

- A home page (which contains a paragraph or so about the company and what we do)
- A page for each book, accessed from the home page by clicking on a photo of the book cover. This page will give a cover shot, a synopsis, any reviews etc, and a 'click to order' button.
- A 'contact us' page with an 'email us' option
- A 'join our mailing list' page (stating a preference between email and snail mail)

We went to see the manager of our local branch of Ottakars yesterday, which was very useful. Here are Rich's notes on the meeting:

We needed to ask various questions relating to returns and how a bookshop within a chain orders.

> Q: *How do you decide which books to order?*
> A: We have a core stock of books which we must stock. These are dictated to us by head office. We can then also choose books to add to this core stock from a variety of sources

including reps, buying online from our intranet facility which recommends titles etc and buying direct from publishers, perhaps as part of a local promotion or publicity as well as the usual buying from the wholesalers.

(From this we got the intranet manager's name and phone number, and a phone call is already on its way to him to find out more.)

Q: *How do you deal with returns?*
A: Any books not sold are returned after around 2 to 3 months. We stock take every two months (not the whole store in one go but section by section) so any books not sold are returned. We try not to over stock but are aware that some reps will try and push too many books on us. Our advice is to tell reps not to do this as it is pointless.

Q: *If your customers are coming in and asking for a particular book do you know why?*
A: Not usually. We might pick up on a local publicity coverage such as Nicola de Pulford's coverage in Devon Life for her Nursery Rhymes book but that is really a one off. Other coverage includes regional press and Radio 4. Regional and local coverage seems to get the best response, even if the book doesn't have a local connection.

Other points covered during discussion were:
Publisher's image not that important although if they are 'difficult' it might sway a buyer into not buying from them. We should concentrate on the books.

Mailshotting book shops not worth the expense nor is faxing.

They get loads of mailshots and generally bin them. However, Andrea said this would work if the books were relevant to her, but the mailshotting is generally poorly targeted.

They don't seem to be that up on their own business. Quite surprised how little they knew – such as upcoming trends, what digital printing is all about, what motivates customers to buy a particular book, why customers are ordering a book, etc.

Customers are likely to come in clutching a web page from Amazon and ask for the book at the shop rather than placing order online – interesting – still a fear of credit card fraud?

Cover design very important.

Matt finish is fine – classier, not that subject to marking.

Sales of *Men are from Mars* gone down since cover redesigned.

We, as White Ladder, must look very professional – we knew this anyway!

GOLDEN RULE: *Get your hands dirty.* No one but you can do your market research. It's your direct involvement in the details of researching and launching the business which will ensure its success.

8 August

We're now wondering whether we should publish *The Voice of Tobacco* first and *The Family Business* (which needs a better title) second. The reason is that we think *The Voice of Tobacco* may generate more attention because it's the kind of book that isn't simply interesting and useful, but also grabs you at a gut level. We're going to have to consult our editorial board on this one. We'll need to put together a marketing plan for each title to show them and encourage them to tell us which they think is the most promising.

We're starting to feel that we're being sucked (willingly) into the White Ladder thing, and it's going to happen. We're not actually committed in any way yet, but neither of us would be happy backing down. We're putting quite a lot of time into it – maybe a couple of hours a day on average – but of course we have to keep earning so we're not giving up the day job.

14 August

Rich is in the process of drawing up a draft contract. The more fully it's done before we show it to a legal expert, the less we presume they'll need to charge us to OK it.

We heard back from Pedalo, the website designers. They've quoted around £3,000 to get us up and running. However, we can knock about £1,000ish off that if we don't do credit card ordering online, but take secure credit card details and then verify offline. We can

to online ordering and verification as soon as we can 'll need to get a PDQ machine from our bank, which . There are more costs than you might think in the ...sign:

- Design, develop and build
- Webhosting
- Secure webspace for credit card transactions
- Email provision
- Mailing list integration and maintenance
- Basic search engine submission
- Website statistics

The statistics mean we can see who is visiting the site, which pages they visit, and how many of them there are. The mailing list means we invite people to submit their details so that we can start to build up a direct mailing list.

I've asked Pedalo to requote more exactly with the revised ordering system. And to let us know what it will cost to design our logo at the same time as the website. So far we're very impressed with them, and other websites we've seen that they've designed look terrific. Clean, professional and fast to download.

Meanwhile, we also had a quote from the printers, Bath Press. This was, surprisingly, almost exactly the figure we'd budgeted. If we print 2,000 copies, on decent paper and with a matt laminated cover (which we prefer to gloss), it will cost us just under £2,000. If we were to print an extra thousand it would put the price up by £500. So that's good.

GOLDEN RULE: *Remember that your website is a big part of how you promote your brand.* If you need a website, build it into your initial design thinking. Don't add it later as an afterthought. Even if you can't afford to set it up now, you can still plan it.

15 August

Great meeting with Mark Allin yesterday, who came all the way to see us for the day – 3 hours' drive each way – just to give us advice. I hope we're that generous with our time when other people need it. And his advice was invaluable. He knows more than any of our other contacts – except perhaps Susan – about the nitty-gritty, practical details for a start. When you need to get your ISBN number sorted out for a new book, how you deal with wholesalers (who are very powerful in the publishing industry) and so on.

As well as all sorts of varied advice and encouragement, he came up with a few especially helpful points, such as:

- How to forecast sales, as far as possible. It has to be a guess, especially to start with, but he agreed with our view that we should be able to sell ten thousand copies in the first year and five thousand in the second. And he gave us an idea of how we could expect those figures to be distributed over the twelve months of each year – essential information for our cash flow forecast.
- If we can get a couple of titles ready in time for the Frankfurt Book Fair in October, Mark (Hayward – our agent as writers, who will

also act for White Ladder) may well be able to sell foreign rights for us there. This could bring in a few thousand pounds with which to pay for the launch of the first book.

We don't feel we can budget for foreign rights sales at this stage – they're such a hit and miss thing – but it would be great to have some income before we incur any significant expenses.

16 August

Good meeting this morning with our accountant, Graham Howe, whom Rich found by asking a solicitor friend for a recommendation. He seems very sharp – just what we need. We warmed to him in particular when he admitted that he actually finds most accounting rather boring (a very clever technique for attracting clients).

He came up with some very useful advice, such as issuing Rich and me with identical shares, but one lot termed A shares and the other B shares. This means that we don't have to pay dividends to both of us at once – we can pay either A *or* B if we want to. So if one of us needs a cash injection before the end of the financial year, but the other is already paying tax (on personal earnings) at 40% and wants to wait for a lean year to earn a dividend, we have that option.

It turns out that having registered the company, we need to change certain things. We registered it with 100 shares and we actually need far more, and we need both A and B type. In fact, we might also have C shares for any future shareholders. We need far more shares – ten thousand or a million, it doesn't really matter so long as it's big – so we can issue them in very small quantities if we ever need to. Otherwise we can never give away less than one percent of the company.

Since we never returned the registration documents (we were waiting until we'd spoken to Graham), we've decided to leave them to expire and let Graham register the company for us. He's quoted £135 to do it, which seems worth it, since he'll get all the details correct. I know it's not essential to have professional financial advice but, even with Rich's background in finance, I wouldn't want to set up the business without a proper accountant.

20 August

Things are beginning to happen.

Mark Hayward is happy to try to sell foreign rights for us at the Frankfurt Book Fair, which is at the beginning of October. As well as proposals and so on, we need to give him some promotional material. We've decided the best thing would be to get the book covers designed and the back cover copy written – that means the work won't be wasted as we'll need it eventually anyway. Mark can print off dummy covers (in full colour) to take with him. One of the books may need a new cover actually – we probably want a photo eventually – but at least we'll have something we can use for now.

If we're getting the covers done, we'll need a logo so we can use the symbol on the spine. So that means we also need to get our logo designed. This is being done by Pedalo, and we've asked them to have it ready by 13th September. It'll be a little more costly than getting a local designer to do it, but it will work well on the website having been designed by the same people.

So we're actually starting to spend money, if only in relatively small amounts. The logo design is costing us £250, and the covers should be another £2-300 between them. This means opening a bank account and starting to feel like a proper business.

I suppose we're committed to White Ladder now, in as much as you're ever committed to a business. Obviously we could get out any time in theory. But I think we've reached the point where we both know we're going ahead. We haven't discussed it in so many words because we don't need to. It's a bit like walking down a steep, muddy slope. Each individual step doesn't seem liike much but there comes a point when, looking back up, you can see how far you've come and it's obvious you ain't going back.

It's a bit scary, but in a fabulous, exciting way. There's no way I'd back out now and I know Rich wouldn't either. We're having too much fun.

24 August

The cash flow forecast is done – and indicates that we should have a viable business. The profit at the end of year one (after we've paid out royalties) is about £10,000 and after year two about £50,000. Of course it's all slightly scary since there are inevitably so many guesstimates in there. But we've got our figures as accurate as we can. It's the sales forecast that we really can't get firm figures for. But the sales forecast of course feeds directly into the income line of our cash flow forecast. However, we can't lose more than about seven or eight thousand pounds, and that's the key thing. We can afford that in the worst case scenario, without going bankrupt.

What's more worrying is that we will have to cut back our other earnings. White Ladder may look stable on paper, but we could be in trouble personally. We simply can't write as many books for other publishers – and therefore earn our usual income – if we're putting the time we need to into making White Ladder successful. There's going to be a nerve-wracking gap between the time we cut down on other work, and the point when White Ladder can replace that income.

The cash flow forecast is actually very useful already, even though we haven't started trading yet. It showed up the fact that we should be in the black by month six (including paying off our initial loan to ourselves), but we'll go back into the red again in month eight as we pay for the costs of publishing the second book.

It's also highlighted the fact that if we reprint several books at a time, we'll have cash flow problems the month we pay for that. So we'll need to keep an eye on reprints and stagger them once we have a few titles.

CASH FLOW FORECASTING

A cash flow forecast is very simple to draw up, and it is essential for telling you when you're likely to run into cash flow problems – in plenty of time for you to take avoiding action. We've started with a two year forecast; the idea is to keep rolling it forward as you go so you always have a forecast that takes you at least a year ahead.

All you need to do is to write down the left hand column of your table the expected areas of income (broken down) and the expected areas of expenditure (also broken down into detail). Along the top of the columns you write each month. (Don't panic, you'll get an example in a minute.)

Now fill in, for each month, the money coming in (in the appropriate line) and total it all in the next line down. Do the same for the money going out. At the bottom you put the balance, which is your gross profit for the month. And below this you can put the running total, carrying forward the profit from the month before each time (this is your 'accumulated gross profit' line).

Make sure you list income and expenditure where it really happens. For example, in our line of business, we know that standard payment terms are 90 days, so we have to allow for this. We'll have to pay our printers and designers and so on on 30 days, however.

Typical income sections might include:
- Start-up capital
- Cash from sales
- Cash from debtors
- Sales of assets
- VAT
- Start-up grant

Typical expenses might be broken down into:
- Payments to suppliers
- Purchases
- Wages
- Commission

- PAYE/NIC
- VAT
- Rent
- Business rates
- Heating/lighting
- Phone/fax
- Stationery
- Transport
- Advertising/promotion
- Professional advisors
- Captial expenditure
- Depreciation
- Loan interest

Over the page you'll see what our first year's cash flow forecast looks like. It's quite simple, and we've broken down our income and expenditure per title we publish since this is more useful for us – and that's what cash flow forecasts are for after all: to be useful. We've also put in a total column at the end, mainly as a way of double checking that all the figures really do add up.

YEAR 1 WHITE LADDER

	Mar	Apr	May	June	July	Aug	Sept	Oct	Nov	Dec	Jan	Feb	
Title 1 Income				3897	3897	3897	1948	1948	1948	1948	1948	1948	23379
Title 2 Income										3897	3897	3897	11691
Title 3 Income													3
Title 4 Income													4
TOTALS	0	0	0	3897	3897	3897	1948	1948	1948	5845	5845	5845	35070
Ex's													
Production T1	0	-3250	0	0	-2000	0	-2000	0	0	-2000	0	0	-9250
Production T2	0	0	0	0	0	0	0	-3250	0	0	-2000	0	-5250
Production T3												-3250	-3250
Production T4													
Acc/legal	0			-1000	0	0	0	0	0	0	0	0	-1000
Travel/stat/sundries	0	-325	-325	-325	-325	-325	-325	-325	-325	-325	-325	-325	-3575
Website design	-2600	0	0	0	0	0	0	0	0	0	0	0	-2600
Totals Ex's	-2600	-3575	-325	-1325	-2325	-325	-2325	-3575	-325	-2325	-2325	-3575	-24925
Gross Profit	-2600	-3575	-325	2572	1572	3572	-377	-1627	1623	3520	3520	2270	10145
Acc Gross Profit	-2600	-6175	-6500	-3928	-2356	1216	839	-788	835	4355	7875	10145	

GOLDEN RULE: *You can't start a business without a proper cash flow forecast.*

8 September

Whoopee! We've just come back from a week's holiday in Cornwall. We arrived back to samples of our new logo from Pedalo, and sample covers from Julie for the first two books. Very exciting. Pedalo gave us three ideas for logos, two of which we hate and one of which we really like. We have the odd minor tweak, but it's looking good.

Julie's covers are terrific, too. Again, we need a bit of tweaking but we're really pleased and very confident we'll end up with what we want. One of them is pretty well there – the parenting book is proving a little trickier.

While we were in Cornwall we went to visit a printer in Padstow, TJ International (recommended by Mark Allin). We asked them to show us around the printing works, so we could see how a book is put together from start to finish. We feel we need to understand the process better in order to appreciate what information printers need, why they have the schedules they do, and why certain options are more expensive than others. Andy Vosper, the Sales Director, showed us round and was extremely helpful. The visit was fascinating, and also very useful. They said they would have a quote in the post for us when we got home – and they did. It's several hundred pounds cheaper than Bath Press, too.

Interestingly, we also had an email from Pedalo saying that they now

TIME ELAPSED 3 months 1 weeks 1 days

have a system for giving us full online payment facilities for about £800 less than their original quote. This is still a few hundred more than the quote for online payment with offline authorisation. But maybe we could offset the cheaper print price against the reduced extra cost of full online payment. Hmm.

GOLDEN RULE: *Learn everything you can about your industry.*

12 September

We met the bank manager today (a relatively easy meeting since we're not asking for a loan). So we now have a White Ladder bank account. We also have a finalised logo, so we really feel like a proper company. All we need now is stationery, which we'll sort out soon. We're waiting for details like our VAT registration number, which our accountant is sorting out. (Since there's no VAT on books it makes sense to register from the start.)

REGISTERING FOR VAT

You won't necessarily want to register for VAT until you have to – which is when your turnover hits a preset level, currently around £55,000. However, you can register below this level if you want to. Charging VAT and then paying it over to the VAT office also entitles you to claim back any VAT you pay your suppliers. In our case, this is a bonus because books are zero rated for VAT (not to be confused with 'tax exempt' or you'll upset the VAT people). This means we don't have to charge VAT and therefore pay it over, but by registering we can still claim back any VAT we pay our suppliers. So we get a cheque from the VAT office every quarter.

If you're going to register for VAT and you have an accountant, they can sort this out for you. If not, all you have to do is contact your local VAT office and they send you the forms. It's as simple as that. You do have to keep your accounts scrupulously up to date and send in your completed VAT return every three months, but they send you a form which serves as a reminder.

There are two relatively recent changes to VAT legislation which affect small businesses:

- Annual accounting, which allows you to send in the paperwork only once a year. You make several interim payments during the year, and one balancing payment with your return. New businesses are generally eligible if their annual turnover is likely to be less than £100,000 (but don't take my word for it – check with your VAT office).

- The flat rate scheme, under which you pay tax on your sales at a flat rate below 17.5% (the rate depends on your industry). The flip side of this is that you can't claim back any VAT, except for single expenditure items over £2,000. This hugely simplifies the accounting process, and may also leave you better off. You're eligible if your taxable turnover will be under £100,000 in the next year, or your total income will be under £125,000 (but again, ask your local tax office).

We've decided we will go ahead with the full online ordering software from Pedalo – it makes sense, otherwise we'll have to pay them to design an order form anyway, which will become obsolete as soon as we upgrade. Which we'll have to do within about a year.

The cover design for the give up smoking book was terrific. Black, white and red and designed like an old-fashioned cigarette packet. Just as we were about to give Julie the go-ahead on it, Rich was browsing on Amazon and found another book with an almost identical cover design – also a book about giving up smoking designed like a fag packet, in red, black and white. Although the content was different, the cover was ludicrously similar, even using a diamond shape in the middle with the title printed on it like ours. What's more, they printed a 'government health warning' on the cover, which we'd been going to do. And their promotional copy compared the price of the book to the price of a packet of cigarettes (we're printing *Cheaper than a couple of packets of fags* under the price on the back cover).

So back to the drawing board. We can't see why we shouldn't use the same basic idea. We think it's great, and we arrived at it entirely independently. However, we're changing the colour from red to green, and swapping the diamond shape for a circle or an oval. And dropping the health warning.

The covers for the parenting book (latest title: *Kids Inc*) were harder to design. We'd really wanted a photo of a small child (one of ours would do fine) dressed in a completely outsized pinstripe suit and tie. But professional photographers can cost upwards of £250 a day, and we simply can't afford it at the moment. So we thought we'd come up with another idea for now (for Mark to take to the Frankfurt Book Fair) and maybe think about designing a new cover with a photo for when we actually publish.

Trouble is, none of us has actually thought of a really good idea even just for now. Julie's put together some very slick covers with reasonable ideas behind them, but they just don't jump out at us. So we reluctantly decided we might have to find a photographer after all and see if we could afford it.

But where to find a good photographer (in South Devon)? It's all wedding photographers and the like, and while some are great, some are crap and you've no way of knowing which you've got until they've taken the photos... and you've incurred the cost. Then we remembered that last year Jack and Ned's school photos were far better than the usual portrait of your child wearing a fixed, fake smile. The photographer had got them looking happy and relaxed and genuinely smiling. So we decided to try to find the woman who took them.

She was tricky to track down – via the school, and she'd moved house. However, we found her after a couple of days and she's coming over with all her lights and equipment to take the photos here at the weekend. And the cost? Just £25 plus the usual cost of prints that we pay for the school ones. We should have gone for that option from the start. In fact, there's a useful lesson here. If you've got an ideal fixed in your mind, you might as well go for it because you'll just be disappointed in every other route you try. We could have saved poor Julie some time if we'd stuck with our instincts. Still, at least we've learnt for next time.

> **GOLDEN RULE:** *Listen to your gut feeling.* It may not be right every time, but it often is. So you need to follow through your gut ideas and find out if they're really as unworkable as they may seem at first.

21 September

Judy, the photographer, turned up and was great. She took a roll of photos, and then took some on Rich's digital camera too (in case there's a delay getting hers developed and we run out of time). There were some excellent digital ones. Yesterday she called round with the contacts from the roll of film she shot, and they're great. At least three really good ones.

Meanwhile, we'd emailed Julie the best digital photos so she could get on and design the cover. She can then easily drop in the final photo once she has it, in place of the digital one. She's come up with a terrific cover design which we're really pleased with. We've also got an endorsement from John Cleese on the cover (nice to have the odd string to pull) which we're extremely grateful to him for, since he's the ideal person to endorse a book which combines business and families. Hopefully his endorsement will give us some credibility too.

22 September

We have an annexe to our house which we hope to use as offices for White Ladder. Only we let it out at the moment and we can't yet afford not to. I asked Rich to look at the figures and see when White Ladder could afford to move in there – paying rent to replace at least some of our present rental income from the tenants, and paying the bills too. He says if our figures work out and sales are as predicted, we could move in there at the end of next year.

This is good news because one of our knottiest problems is logistics. Rich and I have separate phone lines and offices at opposite ends of our rambling old house. This means we're not really in a position to hear – and therefore answer – each other's phones. Since for a lot of the time only one of us is at work while the other looks after the kids, we need to sort this out, otherwise we'll look like an amateur business run from home, and not a professional outfit.

We've decided to use my phone number as the main number for White Ladder. This is because if Rich has a cordless phone on my number in his sitting room (we have separate sitting rooms), he can take it into his office when I'm not around to answer it. Whereas I have no way of answering his phone. Then we can print his number as a direct line to him on our stationery.

We also have to keep our computers separate, although obviously we can email. But once we're in a position to move into our annexe we can have a single phone number and a dedicated White Ladder computer (as well as our own).

GOLDEN RULE: *The smaller you are, the more professional you have to look.*

We've been thinking about all the software we're going to need:

- Sage accounting (with a facility for calculating royalties)
- Adobe Photoshop so I can open any artwork files
- Some kind of database we can enter all our direct customers into, and subsequently select them by region, amount they've spent, frequency of ordering, those who've ordered a specific title and so on. We need this right from the start, as we don't want to have to re-enter a backlog of customers onto a new database later. Even as

few as a hundred could take hours and hours to re-enter with all the info we need.

23 September

Trying to set up a couple more meetings with bookshop managers. I called the book department manager of our local branch of WH Smith. She was very sweet but said she couldn't really help. They are told exactly what books to stock and have no control at all, except for a very small budget for local books. I asked if she chose where to place the books on the shelves, but she told me she was obliged to follow a strict 'planogram' (I assume this must be waffle-speak for a 'plan').

25 September

We went to London yesterday for our first editorial board meeting (doesn't that sound grand?). It would be hard to find a group of five more positive and smart people to advise us. They were full of ideas, and we had a great time. We also had the huge advantage of a stonkingly good meal at The Cinnamon Club in Westminster, a restaurant which also has a great atmosphere for a meeting.

Most importantly, they helped us make some crucial decisions. They loved both books, which was a relief. If they hadn't we'd have been a bit stumped – we obviously don't have to take their advice, but we can't see the point of having them if we're not going to listen to them. Oddly enough, they had few comments on the book we were most concerned about, and more on the one we thought we were happy with. The comments weren't to do with the content, but things like titles and cover designs – all fixable.

They changed the title of *Kids Inc* to *Kids & Co* (well, we changed it, but under their advice). They mostly loved the cover – just a few tweaks. They didn't, however, like the title *The Voice of Tobacco*, so we're going to have to change it. They felt it needed to be clearer what the book was about. We're now researching their views on calling it *Thank You for Not Smoking*. They also felt the cover needed to be much more in-your-face. Colours were the big thing, so we're going back to red and we're going to use it with gold and black (it costs more to print in gold, by about 5p a copy, but if it sells more books it should be worth it).

They also feel that *Kids & Co* is a much more sure-fire seller (although *Thank You for Not Smoking* has great potential too), so that's the one we should publish first.

So that's it. We have a book – with a title – and we can get on with having it ready to publish next March.

USING AN ADVISORY PANEL

It's well worth having a panel of people to call on for those decisions you're reluctant to make alone. In our case, there are times we feel that a unanimous decision simply doesn't carry enough weight when there are only two of us. An ideal advisory panel should consist of:

- About half a dozen people – by the time you're there as well you can't have a useful meeting with many more than that.

■ People whose experience covers areas yours doesn't. There may be some things you're naturally very good at, but you still need someone with more – or different – experience. In our case, we have, among our five advisors:

– Two publishers/commissioning editors

– Two people who have set up and run their own businesses

– One exceptionally good strategic thinker

– One very experienced and talented publishing sales and PR person

– One writers' agent with experience of a wide range of publishing fields

This, of course, adds up to more than five because some people have experience as more than one of these things.

■ You also need people who are both generous with their time and naturally enjoy being involved in new ideas and projects. They're doing this for fun, not for any gain. They may be friends or even family, or they may simply be professional contacts; either way you need to like each other or they won't be motivated.

Once you've got your advisory panel, they need to meet. This not only means you can pick their brains, but it also means that they will feel more involved, more part of the team. It is a bonding exercise; this bond is the only thing keeping them on the panel. You can't expect them to meet endlessly; in our case we'll probably meet three or maybe four times a year. It could be once a month, depending on what you need and how much time your advisors have available to put in.

When you do meet, here are a few guidelines to follow:

■ Treat the meeting professionally: circulate an agenda and

any necessary papers in advance so they can come prepared.

- Don't ask or even encourage them to discuss details – they're there for the big stuff. In our case that means which books to publish, how to present them and ideas for marketing channels to pursue. It doesn't mean asking them whether we should put our page numbers at the bottom or the top on our books, or how we should design our comp slips. With only a couple of hours to spend, we don't want to use it up on anything we could do without them, nor make them feel their time is being wasted.
- Make it enjoyable. We do this by treating them to a slap-up restaurant meal, but you could equally well cook them a meal at home, or take them down the pub and buy them a few rounds. Or even take them out somewhere fun after the meeting.
- Don't feel guilty making them work through a good meal; they know it's what they're there for and they're happy to do it. What they don't want is to feel that they aren't being utilised properly.

Once your advisory panel is established, you can also call or email them individually for anything specific you need their advice on between meetings. Maybe just one of them, or maybe you can send a round robin email or phone several of them – it depends on the particular question. They will be happy to help you, so long as you don't take advantage. Always remember that they're doing this for fun. If they feel they're being pestered it will stop being fun.

Finally, once they're on board, keep them posted of significant developments so they feel involved. In our case this will mean emailing them good news such as striking a big deal of some kind, sending them an advance copy of each book, and otherwise keeping them involved and informed.

We've been discussing the balance of work between Rich and me, and we reckon he should do most of the selling. We can split the PR, but I'm going to be very busy with all my stuff so it makes sense for him to handle the sales.

Thing is, Rich has done plenty of selling before and is a natural in many ways, but he hasn't ever sold a product he didn't have in his hand. While many of the people we want to sell books through can't really be approached until we have the finished book, there are some we will need to talk to in advance. If we want them to put the book in their catalogue, for example, they'll need to make a decision in time to get the entry into the catalogue before it's printed, and so on. So we have to go to them with a manuscript, a cover design and so on, but no actual book.

Rich is very nervous of doing this; he's worried they won't want to deal with him without a final product to look at, and it will put them off coming back to us later. I don't believe this will happen (so long as we select carefully which companies we'll approach in advance), but I can appreciate his worry.

So we're considering printing the first book – Kids & Co – early so that Rich can take it around with him to sell it. In other words we still publish in March, but we have finished copies by January. With any subsequent book our cash flow won't allow us to design and print before we need to, but on the first book it makes less difference. We're putting in our own money, and it doesn't much matter when we transfer it into our White Ladder account, bar a small amount of interest it would have made us personally if we left it where it is for a couple of months longer. But if it helps Rich to get into his stride selling, it will be well worth it.

This tactic could also help avoid any last minute cock-ups when our inexperience could prevent the book being ready for the publication date we've announced. We have to get the books to our distributor, and then to the wholesalers, who need it sometime in advance of the official publication date... all in all a kind of dry run with the first book could help us identify the potential mistakes without actually having to make them.

30 September

Rich is very unsure about changing the title of *The Voice of Tobacco* since it describes exactly what the book is all about. It's odd that we never doubted this title; it was the other one we were worried about. Anyway, various suggestions have been flying backwards and forwards by email, and we're also looking at changing the subtitle (currently *The diary of a not smoker*) instead of the title. We can't apply for the ISBN number until the title is finalised.

2 October

Well, we seem to have sorted out the phone problem. BT apparently have a service which entails putting in an extra line to the house, from which we can run as many extensions as we need. Using these extensions, we can get whichever one we want to ring first, and another to ring if that one is busy or doesn't answer. We can transfer calls to each other and divert calls to mobiles and so on. And of course we have a dedicated business number with its own answerphone and all the rest of it. You can use virtually any phones, but of course if you pay BT £80 they'll sell you a phone which makes it all easy – otherwise you have to learn endless codes using the star and hash keys.

For reasons I completely fail to understand, it took about two hours on the phone (over several calls) to get answers to all our questions – not helped by the fact that every time you call you're on the phone for about five minutes before you ever get to hear a human voice. However, it seems to have been worth it in the end. The total cost – for installing the line and buying two phones – is around £350. As it's exclusively a business service, we have to pay the business line rental rate, which is £55 per quarter. For this we get an entry in the Yellow Pages, as BT like to keep telling us. I wonder how many publishers get worthwhile business through the Yellow Pages. ("I'm bored. I fancy reading a book. Now where can I find one? Hmmm. I know, I'll look up 'publishers' in the Yellow Pages.")

This unbudgeted cost prompted me to take another look at our start-up figures. I never really expected them to stay static – I knew other costs would creep in. As well as the phones we have to pay for ISBN numbers for the books (a bit under £70), and we have to pay our accountant for setting up the business. Our website costs went up a bit too, when we decided to go for the online payment system. On the other hand, our print costs are slightly below budget, and our stationery printing costs will come down because we've decided to stop being silly and just have ordinary business cards.

Anyway, all told our current start-up figure is £6,550 – only a few hundred above the original figure, which is extremely encouraging. However, good as it is for White Ladder, this is our money and WE WANT IT BACK. We're lending it to White Ladder, not giving it, and we need to see a return on our investment.

We're going through a slightly frustrating couple of days at the moment – I have several things I can't get on with until we have certain information. I need the new phone number, the VAT registration number and the company registration number, all of which we should have sorted in the next day or two (Graham, our accountant, is on the case with the last two). Until we have these I can't:

■ Order stationery
■ Apply for ISBN numbers (they need the VAT reg) – every book must have an ISBN
■ Send out the requisite 'title notification sheet' for *Kids & Co* which goes round the industry – wholesalers, online booksellers, trade publications, Book Data industry listings etc – and which requires the ISBN number, for which I can't apply until I have the VAT number

We're getting to the stage of needing stationery, so we want to get on with this. However, a limited company is legally required to put certain information on the letterhead. Without this info we can't print it.

TIME ELAPSED **4** months **0** weeks **2** days

LEGAL REQUIREMENTS FOR LETTERHEADS

If you're a limited company, your letterheads must display the following (somewhere on the page – it doesn't have to be at the top):

■ Full company name (including the Ltd bit – if this isn't in your logo you must print it in full somewhere else)

■ Registered number

■ Registered address

It's not compulsory to print directors' names, but if you do you must print all of them. I can't really see why you'd want to do anything else, but if you do have a director who insists on remaining anonymous then you can't print any of the directors' names.

We only need letterheads, comp slips and business cards at the moment. I have a colour printer so I can print off things like press releases with our logo in colour at the top of it, rather than pay to have that kind of stationery printed.

We're having comp slips in portrait format rather than landscape (i.e. tall and thin) because it leaves more space to write on.

Rich is going to talk to the Sage software advisor at our accountants to find out what happens about Sage compatible accounts stationery. In other words, we want to be able to produce invoices and receipts with White Ladder's details on them. Can the computer churn these out? Or do we have the basic paperwork printed and then print off the invoices etc onto it? We don't know, but we'll find out...

After exchanging emails with Mark Allin and Elie in particular, and brainstorming every spare moment, we've reached a decision on the title of *Thank You for Not Smoking*. We're reverting to the original title, *The Voice of Tobacco* but changing the subtitle to A dedicated smoker's diary of not smoking. We felt *Thank You for Not Smoking* could be the title of a sanctimonious give-up smoking guide, which this emphatically is not. Rich's views on keeping the original title were very strong, and the general consensus was that a change of subtitle should be enough to establish what the book was about. Let's hope we're right.

> **GOLDEN RULE:** *Keep it simple.* Don't waste money on fancy stationery and the like. Put what money you have into the product or your customer service, where it will actively encourage sales.

3 October

Phones. It's like wading through treacle. Every time we phone up we get told something different. However, we now have enough information to be sure we want to go ahead, so we've booked BT to put in this extra line next week. In theory, we're allowed to choose a number we like from the next batch or so coming up for grabs – so we can pick a memorable one. In practice, however, our exchange has only six available numbers, none of them consecutive. So we've chosen three: 813343 (that'll be the 'memorable' one), 814118 (my direct number) and 814124 (Rich's direct number). That's what you get for living in the sticks.

Yesterday we went to see the owner/manager of one of our local independent bookshops, Torbay Books in Paignton, and took him to lunch to pick his brains. We were absolutely delighted to find that he's not just a bookshop owner. He used to be a publisher. He worked for lots of companies – Mitchell Beazley, Hamlyn, Octopus, Reader's Digest, David & Charles – working his way up to sales and marketing director.

His name's Matthew Clarke; he's a great guy and very encouraging. We were pleased because he started off saying he often had people approach him for advice on starting out in publishing, and he always advises them not to. He warned us that he was likely to do the same with us. But by the time we'd talked about White Ladder for twenty minutes or so, he told us he actually thought in our case that we had the potential to be successful. He was impressed with how well we'd thought it all out, and despite our background as writers he was persuaded that we understood marketing too.

I'm sure we'll stay in touch with Matthew. I think he'll enjoy the occasional chinwag about White Ladder as much as we'll appreciate his advice. And anyway, we liked him and would like to keep in touch.

4 October

I got so fed up waiting for our VAT number to come through that I phoned the ISBN agency, who tell me we can apply without it. It's requested on the form but it's not essential. I wish I'd bothered to phone sooner. Still, I've now applied for our ISBN numbers. As far as the book industry is concerned, a book might as well not exist if it doesn't have an ISBN. The big wholesalers and bookstores simply won't deal with books which don't have an ISBN. As far as I can gather, their computerised systems rely on the ISBN to access information about the book.

Until the ISBN for *Kids & Co* comes through, I can't notify the book industry that the book is being published. I need to send out information to the wholesalers, big bookstores and a few other organisations such as Book Data, who circulate information on new titles to all the bookstores.

Once an ISBN is allocated to a book, you can't change the title or subtitle, or change the binding (as in softback to hardback or vice versa) without notifying everyone all over again. So we have to be sure what title and so on we want to use.

We've decided that we *will* make our books available thorugh all the usual bookstores as well as via other channels too, so sorting out ISBNs and so on is important.

8 October

Rich has set up online banking with HSBC so that he can check White Ladder's account online, pay regular bills online and get statements and so on. This was a nightmare to set up. It involved filling in a very detailed form and then taking it to a local branch where he had to present his passport and have the form certified as having been filled out by him. Then he had to send it off, and was later sent more information (in the post, not online). This gave him the web address. Then he had to go online and fill in another whole set of forms which took ages. Eventually he got to the bank site, and to our own account.

Now it's all set up he can access our account quite quickly. It's just getting there that was a real pain in the ass. I don't remember any of this trouble with my personal First Direct account (and they're owned by HSBC).

Also, Rich has enquired about Sage compatible stationery. It does exist, but it's extortionately expensive – at least it seems it to us. It's probably well worth it to people with bigger budgets than ours, but we'll have to find an alternative. We really can't afford to keep spending another £50 here or £200 there. With our earnings about to drop dramatically we need to spend only what is really essential.

12 October

Yesterday we went to see the manager of one of the branches of Waterstones in Exeter. He was very helpful generally, and answered all our questions. He tells us they buy through reps, and order direct from publishers (at a 40-50% discount). They only use Bertrams (one of the big wholesalers) to place single orders for customers. He pointed out that if we don't use reps, they won't stock the book. If customers come in asking for it after hearing about it in the media, Waterstone's can order it for them, but they won't have a copy on the shelf the customer can just pick up and buy.

So should we find a good rep to sell our books for us? Reps take a sizeable percentage of sales (usually 10%), so will it be cost effective for us? Waterstones now see very few freelance reps (those that represent

a number of smaller publishers simultaneously), so we'd have to find
a good one whom Waterstones will actually see. In fact, we need to
find several to cover the whole country. Rich is going to look into it.
Meanwhile, Waterstones in Exeter kindly gave us the phone number
of the one they deal with round here.

SAGE ACCOUNTING

Rich is getting to grips with Sage accounting (rather him than
me). It seems to be the system to use. He says when he first
used it about 15 years ago he found it unhelpful and tricky so
he was reluctant to use it for White Ladder. But he's been surprised to find that it's very easy to use now and a bit like windows.

It costs £110 to buy the package and have it installed by an
accountant, plus £100 for half a day's training. It will do VAT
returns, compile reports, do double entry bookkeeping, trial
balance, nominal ledger, profit and loss and calculate royalties
for us. You can do a profit and loss for the whole company or
just for one product. Sage also promote their online support
system (at around £100) but Rich reckons this probably isn't
worth it when our accountants have installed it and offer the
same service. It might well be worthwhile if you didn't have an
accountant.

BT have installed our phones. They're working fine and the system
is well worth having. BT did manage to knock down a chunk of our
guttering in the process of installing the lines, though. When I
phoned up to ask for recompense for this – which obviously
involved being transferred, talked to by machines and given different numbers to ring countless times – I was surpised to discover

TIME ELAPSED **4** months **1** weeks **5** days

(eventually) that BT appears actually to have a whole department which exists purely to sort out claims from customers for damage done by their engineers.

14 October

Rich has spoken to the rep Waterstones recommended, and he's coming to see us on Wednesday. I've looked at the figures and worked out what the maximum discount we can sell at is before we actually lose money on the sale. Breakeven, in other words.

Our first print run of 3,000 copies could sell at a discount of 85% and still break even – that won't cover start-up costs obviously, nor overheads, and nor will it cover post and packaging (hard to calculate since we don't know what bulk we're likely to despatch in). But it covers direct costs: printing, design, typesetting etc. Subsequent reprints of 2,000 could go up to a discount of 88%.

It's hard to see why we would want to sell at this kind of discount very often, or indeed why we would need to. But it's a useful figure to calculate. If the rep takes 10%, that obviously comes out of that discount.

Now… databases. I feel strongly that we need a really good customer management database. I want to be able to mail – by land or in cyberspace – anyone who has contacted us or bought one of our books direct from us. Since we want to encourage direct sales (cutting out the middlemen and increasing our profits), we need a decent way of storing and using customer information. Then we can build a good relationship with each customer, start a newsletter in a couple of years and so on.

To do all this, I want to be able to select customers from the database by as many criteria as possible so I can, for example:

- Email everyone who hasn't bought from us in the past year
- Mailshot all customers who have bought a particular book and offer them a discount on additional copies
- Email all customers in a particular area about a local or regional event, such as an exhibition we're attending, or a book signing in their area
- Contact everyone who has spent more than a certain amount with us to offer a bonus (such as 50% discount on their next order)

…and so on. The opportunities are endless, but only if we can select customers by all these kinds of criteria. We also need to be able to enter data we collect over the phone or by post, and the data that comes via our website.

We don't necessarily need all this now. But suppose we get 30 orders a week by post and website (and that's a modest estimate). That means that if we wait only a year to set up a database, we would already have a backlog of 1,500 sets of customer details to enter. What's that going to cost? So it makes sense to set the database up now, even if only in a basic form, but one we can add to later without having to start again from scratch. That way, we keep it up to date as we go along, starting from day one.

So I've been talking to Guy at Pedalo about the options. There are lots of ways to do it, some linked to the website and others not, some more expensive than others, some harder to learn to use, and so on. It looks as though the most basic system they could put together, which would do what we want, will cost between £1,000 and £1,500 (plus VAT, but we can claim that back). We're going to talk to a couple more people for advice (Elie's put us onto someone who should be a big help), but we reckon we'll go for the most basic system we can and build it up as we can afford it.

CUSTOMER MANAGEMENT DATABASE

It's worth having some kind of database from the start if you're going to have a lot of customers. If you're a consultant with half a dozen key clients you don't need it, but if you're going to have hundreds of customers from the start (and growing) it's the only way to keep track of them and to be able to contact them with customised mailings. The key data to hold is:

- Customer name
- Address
- Postcode
- Email address
- Product ordered + value of order + date (every time they order)
- How the customer made contact (via phone, website, fax, post etc, and also some code to indicate specific mailings, exhibitions etc). This means you can track how new customers come to you
- Contacts from yourself (codes to indicate particular mailings, invitations etc). You can see which approaches work, and you may also want to refer to these contacts when you mail the customer subsequently
- Notes (such as delivery problems, complaints etc)
- Whether or not they're happy to be contacted (you need to ask this especially for email contacts to avoid spamming your customers).

You must register with the Data Protection Registrar if you hold any personal information about customers – even as little as their names and addresses. This applies even if the information isn't stored on computer. There are a few exemptions from this, but often it's easier to register than to keep checking you're still in compliance. You can contact the Data Protection Registrar at: *Information Commissioner's Office, Wycliffe House, Water Lane, Wilmslow, Cheshire SK9 5AX 01625 545745* **www.dataprotection.gov.uk** Registration costs £35 per year.

We plan to let customers know that we will not pass on their details to any other company, since we feel this gives a stronger image and will help strengthen customer loyalty. In any case, although I know it's not the standard marketing line, I personally don't approve of passing on details just because the customer didn't happen to tick a box so small they never noticed it. So I'd feel hypocritical doing it to our customers.

We also plan to suggest that if they don't want us to email them, they don't give us their email address (and therefore giving us the address constitutes permission to use it).

GOLDEN RULE: *Set up and integrate your database right from the start.* If you're starting the kind of business where you're ever going to need a database, you need to find the money to get it in place from the start. As you can see from our experience, it doesn't have to be that expensive.

15 October

I'm feeling pathetically excited this morning, because our ISBN numbers have arrived. This means we can finally get on and tell people the title exists. I shall send out all the notification sheets today.

Rich and I have decided to write out job descriptions for ourselves. So far we haven't fallen out at all over who does what and who has the final say over what. We've had the occasional disagreement, but nothing that any business partners wouldn't – all perfectly reasonable and resolved after an amicable discussion. However, being married to each other does make it more important that we prevent heated arguments, or these could run over into evenings and weekends. In any case it's only common sense to clarify which jobs are whose, otherwise some may be unnecessarily duplicated while others don't get done at all. I've pointed out to Rich that drawing up job descriptions is his job.

It's dawned on us that we need to look ahead. If we want to publish two books next year (one spring, one autumn) and four in 2004, it's time we started thinking about the 2004 titles. The first will publish in the January, which means we need to be ready to go on it by about June of next year (as soon as we're sure *Kids & Co* is selling and we have a viable business). To be ready by June means coming up with the idea, bouncing it off our editorial board informally, putting together a list of marketing ideas, writing a proposal and finding an author... all in time to formalise the decision at our next editorial board meeting in London in February or March.

16 October

The freelance rep that Waterstone's recommended came to see us today. He was very complimentary about our business, our titles and the professionalism of the material we'd put together (I always believe that the smaller you are, the more you have to look professional in order to gain credibility. Since we couldn't be any smaller – with only one book – we've worked very hard to make our material as professional as possible).

In fact, he was an all round nice guy, and very straight. He wasn't sure he could sell enough copies to make it worth our while (or his). He said this was no reflection on our product, but simply our size. We might be better off getting interest via good publicity, and let customers go to the bookshops and ask for the book. It's very difficult to get bookshops interested in new publishers and prepared to take a gamble.

He also said that it would help if we didn't handle orders directly but used a distributor – probably the one who's already handling the warehousing and despatch for us. It gives us more credibility with the wholesalers and the likes of Waterstones, who are reluctant to deal with individual small publishers direct. We have to pay any distributor a cut, which is partly why we've resisted it, but maybe they'll agree to handle orders from the big players in the book trade only, while we handle the rest direct.

Anyway Jim, the rep, likes *Kids & Co* and has taken away the material on it. He's going to show it to a few bookshop buyers and see if he thinks he can sell enough to be worthwhile. Then he'll let us know. He won't start touting it around for a couple of months, since three months before publication is standard for these things.

TIME ELAPSED 4 months 2 weeks 2 days

Meanwhile... Mark Hayward has come back from the Frankfurt Book Fair with quite a lot of interest in foreign rights for *Kids & Co* and *Voice of Tobacco*. Most of his foreign agents want to see the book before they start selling it, but the Italian agent wanted to get cracking on it straight away. It's very confusing – our agent has his own agents overseas. Anyway, he also has several European publishers who might be interested too.

20 October

We've just had a letter from Gardners, one of the big wholesalers, to say they won't be stocking *Kids & Co*. To be honest, I was surprised. Not that they won't be stocking it, but that they took the trouble to write and say so. They say that if there's a demand, they'll be in touch and order it then. So all we have to do is create a demand, and we'll be fine. If we can't do that, we're in trouble anyway.

We've spoken to our warehouse people in the light of the rep's comments about needing a distributor who the wholesalers and big chains are used to dealing with. We spoke to Matthew Clarke at Torbay Bookshop first, who agreed that most independent bookshop owners would rather not bother to stock books they can't order easily through Gardners or whichever wholesaler they use. Anyway, normally our warehouse/distributor either:

- Distributes – where they handle the whole order process and charge us a 15% cut on all orders, or
- Picks and packs only – as they call it, where we handle all the orders and they simply mail out, charging us for labour and p+p only.

They offer one service or the other, but not both to the same customer.

We felt we might need a distributor for the book trade, but we really couldn't afford to give them 15% on all orders, including those outside the book trade. So I called to explain the problem, and ask if they would give us one level of service in the trade, and the other outside it. I spoke to the boss, Allan Lovegrove, who said they'd never been asked to do it before, but he appreciated why we were asking and would find out. He couldn't see why it shouldn't be possible. He'll let us know next week.

23 October

Hurrah! Our VAT number has finally arrived. This means we can go ahead and print our stationery.

I've spoken to our warehouse/distribution company who say it will be possible to give us two levels of service. I'm now going to recirculate the big wholesalers like Gardners, and give them these details. We'll see if it makes them any more willing to deal with us.

I really wanted a media guide to use for PR. It gives you the contact names, addresses and so on of all the newspapers and magazines in the UK, so I know who to send press releases to. They're organised by category, so we can find all the parenting magazines, or all the health publications (for *Voice of Tobacco*).The trouble is, all the media guides (there are several) cost a fortune. We're talking hundreds of pounds. Some are updated and circulated monthly, and some yearly, but even the cheapest is over £150.

So I contacted Helena, who looks after PR at one of my publishers. She very kindly agreed to pass on her out of date media guides as soon as her updated ones come through. I may need to double check a few of the contact details, but that's not a problem. At least the guides will give me the phone numbers so I can check.

> **GOLDEN RULE:** *Beg or borrow if it saves you money.* If it doesn't affect the product and service you give your customers, don't spend money you don't have to.

24 October

I've been investigating getting our books on amazon.co.uk. Obviously we'd rather people bought direct from our own website, but we need to be listed on Amazon as a lot of people will prefer to buy that way. It seems that Amazon offer small publishers two options: join their small publishers' scheme, or have the book listed as 'normally despatches in 6-8 weeks'. The fact that we will actually despatch next day is evidently immaterial.

So it looks like we have to join the scheme. Unfortunately, Amazon's scheme for small publishers includes them buying in books at a non-negotiable discount of 60%. They say that negotiating different discounts with different publishers wouldn't be fair on those who didn't manage to negotiate such a good discount. This seems to me a novel approach to business. I can't think of any other organisation which insists on working to the same terms with all its suppliers rather than risk being unfair. I also can't help feeling that if they really want to be fair to small publishers, they might like to consider buying at a discount small publishers can afford.

However, the fact is that they have us over a barrel. I feel strangely ambivalent to Amazon now. I must be one of their best customers, and as a customer I think they're fantastic. But as a supplier I'm rather going off them. There are few things more infuriating and frustrating than being at the mercy of huge bureaucratic organisations whom you're obliged to deal with.

25 October

Rich has been investigating insurance. We don't need public liability insurance, because we won't have the public visiting our 'offices' (for 'offices' read 'home'). But we think we may need professional indemnity insurance. This will cover us in case, for example, we are sued for breach of copyright in one of our books. The broker Rich spoke to mentioned another kind of insurance called 'home business' insurance, which covers you for things like theft of computers, and the occasional work-related visitor. It's much cheaper than public liability insurance, and far more relevant.

INSURANCE

The only compulsory insurance you need is:

- Employers' liability insurance if you employ any staff
- Motor insurance for any vehicles connected with the business
- Insurance specified in contracts

■ Insurance required by law for specific pieces of equipment

You might also want to consider:

■ Home business insurance, which we're taking out for White Ladder
■ Buildings and contents insurance
■ Insurance against theft
■ Insuring goods in transit
■ Insuring theft of cash
■ Public liability insurance, in case any visiting member of the public is injured
■ Product liability insurance, in case anyone is injured using your products
■ Professional indemnity insurance, if you give advice which you could be sued over. Or, in our case, where an author we commission might unbeknownst to us breach copyright or give negligent or dangerous advice.
■ Keyman insurance, to cover you if one of you is unable to work, or even keyman life insurance (paid to the business, obviously)

This is not an exhaustive list, but includes the types of insurance most likely to apply to a small business.

5 November

My first proper White Ladder phone call on the new phone number. Very exciting. It was from someone at The Bookseller, the publishing trade magazine.

The proofs for *Kids & Co* have arrived, and they look superb. We're so pleased with them – the book's going to look really slick and professional as well as appealing.

10 November

Our agent, Mark Hayward, is leaving the agency – and indeed the profession. He's going to hand over everything to his replacement once they've been appointed. So we're back to square one with selling foreign rights. Bugger.

15 November

Well, recirculating the information about *Kids & Co* with the new distributor's details must have done the trick. Because today we received our first order, from one of the big wholesalers, for three copies. We've framed it.

We didn't really know what to do with it, actually. We don't have a system as yet, least of all a system for handling orders for products which won't be released for another 4 months. Also, this particular wholesaler told us a while back on the phone that their terms were 55% for small publishers. The order arrived with no terms indicated at all, and we're not really happy about giving 55%.

So I called Mark Allin and asked his advice – it's great having helpful people who know what they're talking about on the end of the phone when you need them. He said we should simply accept the order and let them know what our 'terms of trading' were. He reckoned about 45% was entirely reasonable, and they'd probably accept it without any argument. He advised us to talk to our distributor too, who will actually handle orders once the book is published, and ask their policy on discounts. Rich duly called Allan, who agrees that 45% makes more sense, and told us the standard procedure for accepting a book which isn't yet published (just fax back the order marked NYP – 'not yet published'). He also said he'll talk through all these things with us nearer to publication.

19 November

We've found someone who might be interested in selling *Kids & Co* to big corporates. We see it as being ideal for family friendly businesses who could buy it in bulk and give a copy to every employee who has a baby. Cheaper than flowers, lasts longer, is relevant to work and entertaining and useful too. But cold calling businesses is a very time-consuming job. Well, an old friend/work contact, Maggie Tree, has a business which sells into big corporates anyway. She's very happy to have a crack at selling *Kids & Co* alongside her own products, which is great news.

We're in the process of designing an A5 flyer for *Kids & Co*. There's a big bulk printing company who do these things pretty cheap. Printing in full colour on both sides, it's going to cost us just under £350 (including delivery) for 10,000 leaflets. And what will we do with them all? Well, there are various organisations which will put a leaflet in with every mailing. The trick is to find mailings which are going to people as closely matched as possible to our target readership – in this case parents with a disposable income where either the mother works, or the father is involved with the kids (in other words, at least one parent who both works and raises the children). Maggie has also said she'll put a flyer in with every order she sends out. And once we have more books, we'll put a flyer for one of our other books in with every book we mail out.

We've made the back cover of the flyer an order form (the front is a photo of the book and the blurb about it). No point sending out information if we don't give people a chance to send us their money. We've made the ordering process as user-friendly as we can. We also want to collect as much information about customers as we can for our database. Here's what the order form bit of our flyer looked like before our designer got her hands on it (it now says exactly the same but is much better laid out).

KIDS&Co ORDER FORM

Why not order a copy of **KIDS & Co** and discover how much you already know about parenting without realising it? Or you could buy a copy to give someone else.

You can order **KIDS & Co** in any of the following ways:
By phone 01803 813343
By fax 01803 813928
Online at our website **www.whiteladderpress.com**
By email to **enquiries@whiteladderpress.com**
By post to White Ladder Press, Great Ambrook, Near Ipplepen,
Devon TQ12 5UL

We'll normally send your copy out by first class post within 24 hours (but please allow five days for delivery). We don't charge postage and packing.

Title (Mr/Mrs/Miss/Ms/Dr etc) _____

Name _____

Address _____

_____

_____ Postcode _____

Daytime phone number _____

Email _____
(if you prefer to be contacted this way)

I would like to order   copies of **KIDS & Co**
@ £6.99 per copy
                                        TOTAL: £ _____

Please either send us a cheque made out to **White Ladder Press Ltd** or fill in the credit card details below.

Type of card   ☐ Visa   ☐ Mastercard   ☐ Switch

Card number _____

Start date (if on card)   Expiry date   Issue no (Switch)

Name as shown on card _____

Signature _____

We'd really appreciate it if you'd give us a bit more information about yourself. Please would you answer any of the following questions you feel happy to? It's purely for our own records – we never sell or pass on our customers' details to anyone else.

Your email address (we may contact you occasionally, so if you'd rather we didn't please don't give us your address) _____

Where did you receive this order form from? _____

Are you ordering KIDS & Co ☐ for yourself   ☐ for someone else

How many children do you have, and what ages? _____ (number) _____ (ages)

May we contact you about other White Ladder books you might like?   ☐ Yes   ☐ No

27 November

We're ever so excited. This week's issue of The Bookseller, the trade publication which all booksellers and publishers read, contains a preview of paperbacks to be published next March. I submitted info about *Kids & Co*, but the woman who compiles the preview warned me that space was at a premium and she'd be unlikely to be able to include it. But, bless her heart, she did find room for for it. And she gave us a nice little write up: *Kids & Co. Launch title of a new publishing company that aims to select titles with a broad appeal and a quirky angle. This first links bringing up children with sales and management. With an energetic marketing campaign, it could get good coverage.*

6 December

It's a frustratingly inactive time at the moment. The book is at the printers, and it's too soon to start any selling or PR since we've still got another three months to go until publication date. December isn't a good time for getting responses out of people anyway. We've now had our 10,000 flyers printed, and they look terrific – they were delivered this week and it was great opening the boxes and seeing them.

I've been occupying myself typing up addresses from the media guides Helena gave us on to a template so I can print them out onto sheets of address labels. This is a job I don't want to have to do once we're in the thick of things around publication. I have typed around 80 or 90 addresses so far, and I'm about half way through. I've put them into different groups, so I can easily run off just the groups I need for any given book. At the moment, ready for *Kids & Co*, I've got the following groups:

- Parenting magazines
- Other magazines suitable for *Kids & Co* (but not for every parenting title we do in future)
- Business publications
- National press
- Local press
- Regional press (not only round here, but other regions too)

Any time we publish a new title with a different special interest area, I'll add another group of addresses. For example, when we publish *The Voice of Tobacco* I'll go through the health and lifestyle magazines and pick out the ones which look suitable.

We've been taking advice from our distributor, Allan Lovegrove, about establishing a sliding scale of discounts for book trade sales, according to how many copies they buy. We wanted something both reasonably standard and memorable, so for now we've settled on:

1-3 copies: 25%
4-9 copies: 35%
10-99 copies: 45%
100+ copies: 55%

However, we'll take advice.

We seem to be expending a lot of effort on worrying about discounts. The thing is, when we're in a relatively cost-sensitive market which dictates our prices, our profits are going to be dependent entirely on how small a discount we can manage to sell at.

Once we agree a discount with a customer we'll never have any significant scope to reduce it later, so we have to get it right from the start.

I'm also busy writing the copy for our website, so Guy at Pedalo can work on it during January and February. I've been looking at lots of other websites to see what they say. We have only six pages at the moment:

■ Home page
■ *Kids & Co*
■ *The Voice of Tobacco*
■ About us
■ News and offers
■ Mailing list

We had hoped to register domain names for each of our titles, so our publicity could say 'Find it on kids&co.com' or whatever. This address would then forward the user to the relevant page of our website. Unfortunately though, the domain names we want aren't available. In any case you can't put an ampersand in a web address, and the names we want are only available as .net or .co.uk or some other variation. The whole point of the exercise is to make it memorable, so that if people can only remember the title of the book they can still find us online simply by keying in the title plus .com. However, if they have to remember what the suffix is, or that the word 'the' is missing at the beginning, or that 'kids-and-co' is hyphenated or whatever, they might as well just remember whiteladderpress.com.

If the domain names had been available it would have cost about £80 per title for two years, including the forwarding function (Pedalo would have organised it all for us). As it is, we'll pay instead to make sure that if people key in the title on a search engine, the relevant page of our website will come up. Guy's away at the moment, but when he gets back we'll find out what this will cost us.

We've done our best to keep the website clear, simple and friendly. If you want to see what we've done, you can check it out at **www.whiteladderpress.com**

GOLDEN RULE: *Think hard about discounts, because you can't reduce them later.* If your business is going to sell to wholesalers or retailers, you'll need to get the discounts right from the start.

GOLDEN RULE: *When it comes to website design, keep it simple.* It's that Keep It Simple rule again. Unless you're in an industry where it's de rigeur, don't use fancy graphics and animations – they cost too much and people get fed up waiting for them to download.

11 December

Matthew Clarke and his wife, Sarah – ex-publishing people who own the Torbay Bookshop – came to supper the other night. We thoroughly enjoyed the evening, and they agreed to join White Ladder's editorial board. This means that we actually have people on board (so to speak) who deal with real customers – the ones who actually buy books in order to read them.

We have finally sorted out our contracts, with some help from Mark Hayward kindly looking through them for us. We now have standard contracts to issue for authors and editors, and have issued and signed our own contracts for *Kids & Co* and *The Voice of Tobacco*.

17 December

Very exciting news – Anne (our replacement agent) has heard back from *She* magazine. They're not interested in paying for serial rights (which was always a long shot anyway) but they *do* want to run a piece on the book in their April issue which comes out early March. I've talked to the editor concerned, and emailed her a chapter, and she's replied with the text of a very nice little article including a few tips from the book. Our first PR success (thanks to Anne).

I've been sending out press releases and a copy of the cover to all the monthly publications on our list which may be planning their March or April issues already. (I took Elie's advice on this.) I was worried about missing their deadlines if I did nothing until Elie's been down in late January to give me a PR masterclass. The received wisdom is that you don't mail out until you have finished copies of the book available, but Elie says this isn't really essential – on her advice I simply included a covering letter explaining that copies will be available soon and in the meantime here's the basic information in time for spring issues of their magazine.

Anne has just called to say that Junior magazine are very interested in doing something, and may even pay for extracts. I'm particularly pleased with this because Junior is by far the best magazine to be in, and is my favourite parenting magazine (in fact it's the only one I read regularly). She's emailing them the manuscript and we'll see what happens...

Rich has been asking Mark Allin for his advice on discounts. He says a sliding scale is a bad idea, as the wholesalers will be inclined simply to sit on orders until they've clicked over into the next discount bracket. He recommends we have a flat discount of 40% for everyone, but allow the big wholesalers to negotiate us down to 45%. If they want more, we should tell them to leave it at 45% for a year and then look at it again. If they're selling enough, we'll give them a bigger discount. This means they will need to promote the books actively if they want their discount to increase.

While I'm writing this, I've just had a great email from *She* magazine. I'd asked them to let me know if they wanted a cover shot of the book. They're saying yes please, and also can they do a reader offer on *Kids & Co*. This means they offer readers a discount if they phone us direct with the order quoting a reference. It's a good way to get direct orders, and something we wanted to look at doing with magazines generally anyway. So definitely yes.

5 January

Well, back to it after the Christmas break. I've had a call from the printers to say that the books are bound and ready, and should be with us in the next few days. We're getting ever so excited about it.

I've started calling round some of the publications with a couple of months or more lead time, to see if they want to run a piece on *Kids & Co*. It's a laborious process –the person you want to speak to is always out (why is that?) – but it has to be done. Actually, I found the prospect quite scary, and I had to take a deep breath and just pick up the phone. Once I'd made the first call it was fine. I only just started with the first few, and so far it's mostly a matter of finding out when to call people back. I've had one or two say no, very nicely, simply because the book doesn't suit their reader profile. I've also had one or two show a lot of interest and want more information or a copy of the book.

I now have about 150 addresses typed up, ready to print out onto labels, when the time suits to mail each category. But I need more specific records than this, so I've started a card index file for press contacts. Each person I call gets a card, so as I call round I'll gradually build up a working index of active media contacts.

KEEPING PR RECORDS

It's well worth having some kind of system to record your dealings with the media. It means you can quickly look up the details of any publication or programme, and see what your history with them is – what they said yes and no to in the past, whether they like to do special offers, product reviews, features etc, and what their lead times are. You need to record:

- Publication/programme name
- Contact name and job title
- Contact details
- Distribution of the publication
- One line description of their target readership/listeners
- Notes such as what type of stories they look for, or whether they prefer to be contacted by post or email (ask them)
- Each communication by date – a brief summary of the conversation or any action points

File these alphabetically by the name of the programme or publication, and you'll be able to find your way around the system quickly and easily.

> **GOLDEN RULE:** *Plan your PR well in advance.*

I wanted to be able to send emails that give my address at the top as **roni@whiteladderpress.com**, instead of giving my personal email address. After consulting Rich, who has just been through this process himself, it turned out that I could only do it if I installed Outlook Express 6. So I did this (it took a couple of hours to download) and I now have the option, with every email I send, of choosing who it comes from. It seems to have slowed everything down on my computer, unfortunately, but it's still worth it.

6 January

Wow! The books turned up this morning, and they look great. I just keep worrying that I'm about to find a glaring mistake.

I've been phoning around the monthly publications I mailed in December, and getting quite a good response. There are some who say the book doesn't suit their profile; they don't cover that kind of stuff. But those who do all sound interested, and most of them remembered the press release and commented on the fact that it had grabbed their attention and they thought it was an interesting idea. We've even got interest from Tesco Clubcard Magazine, which has a distribution of 7,500,000. I don't know how many of them actually read it, but it must be a fair few.

DISTRIBUTION VS READERSHIP

When you look in media guides and the like, you'll often see the distribution figures listed for publications. While these are a useful indicator of how many people will see your article, they don't tell the whole story. There's a significant difference between distribution and readership:

- Distribution: the number of copies distributed. For some publications, many copies will never be read (for example, all those free local news sheets that come through your letterbox). Unsolicited publications are obviously unlikely to be read by everyone who receives them. Paid for publications, on the other hand, will be read by most if not all of the recipients.

- Readership: this figure is hard to establish and rarely quoted; it refers to how many people a publication is read by. This figure can be higher than the distribution figure, if each copy is read by an average of more than one person. If the magazine is passed round colleagues, friends, family or the dentist's waiting room, this can sometimes be very much higher than the distribution figure.

You need to take these factors into account when you assess the benefits of appearing in a particular publication, either in the editorial or when you buy advertising space. With a bit of thought you should be able to work out in most cases roughly how the readership will relate to the distribution figures.

8 January

Rich found a company in the *Yellow Pages* who make stamps (not postage stamps; stamps for stamping with). We've decided that the best way to organise our stationery – invoices, receipts, delivery notes and so on – is to use off-the-shelf duplicate or triplicate books, and add our own stamp to the top of the page. It's not as classy as having our own stationery, but it's a lot cheaper. And it will still look better than an off-the-shelf receipt book (or whatever) without our details stamped on the top. The stamp has our logo, contact details and company number on it, and we also bought ink pads in a blue as close to our own company shade of blue as we could get. Two stamps and two pads cost us £58 from Stamps Direct in Norwich.

We've had to think through each piece of paper and where it goes in order to work out what we need in dulplicate, triplicate etc. Suppose I take an order at my desk. That order form needs to go to our 'packing station' (a table in Rich's office) for processing, and to Rich for accounting, and to me for entry on the database... We've been through this mental process with all the vital paperwork to make sure we get the stationery we really need.

10 January

I've been to London for a couple of days with Jack and Ned. I came back with orders for three books – one from my sister (for a friend) and two from Rachael Stock whom we saw while we were there.

We've decided we can't afford to give away books to all our family and friends, but we're selling them at £5 instead of £6.99.

Rich has been getting to grips with how we enable customers to pay us by credit and debit card, as well as by cheque. They need to be able to do this both online when they order through the website, and also by phoning or sending us their details. It's an expensive option to offer (at least it seems expensive on our budget) but we feel it's essential.

We feel it's essential to be professional and give customers all the options. Obviously you can refuse to accept credit cards, or you can take details down from the website and then verify them offline (you have to tell the customer you're doing this, because they won't get a confirmation from you online). However, we really feel these kinds of options are for amateurs, and we need to be – and be seen to be – totally professional.

CREDIT AND DEBIT CARD PAYMENTS

The methods of taking credit and debit card payments are totally different online and offline.

Online

You have to use some kind of secure payment system – we're using WorldPay because Guy at Pedalo recommended them. This involves filling in a lengthy form online. Once this is done, they liaise with the website designer who sorts out integrating it into the website.

Fixed costs: set up fee of £75 and then an annual fee of £150 (works out at £12.50 per month)
Transaction costs: 4.5% for credit cards (which is 31p a book

for White Ladder), and 50p per transaction for debit cards such as Switch. There doesn't seem to be a minimum transaction amount.

You can access WorldPay at **www.worldpay.com**

Offline

The only way to do this properly is with a card swipe machine which is plugged into the phone line. You have to get a machine supplied by your own bank (HSBC in our case) so they have you somewhat over a barrel: do it their way, at their price, or you have to move your entire bank account (and I doubt there's that much difference between banks).

This was another long drawn out process. For a start, Rich asked HSBC for the information in early October. Someone from the bank phoned him a few evenings later and, as he puts it, 'machine-gunned' figures at him despite the fact he was trying to give supper to three small children. Unsurprisingly, it didn't all go in. No written back-up material arrived, so in early December he phoned and asked for the information again. After yet another request, they finally got back to him this week.

It's pretty expensive, and if you don't put a minimum of £20 worth of business through it each month they take the shortfall out of your account. (Thanks a bunch – just the sort of encouragement a small business needs.) We have to sign up for an initial term of two years and then it's three months' notice. And, just to twist the knife, we have to buy their till rolls (£8.50 for ten rolls, which should last about a year, apparently).

You have to have a dedicated phone line while the machine is communicating with its Big Brother, although this isn't long so you can always share a line and only key in card details when you're not using the other equipment on the line. Apparently, however, you can't share with a fax line as it corrupts the fax machine or something.

Fixed costs: set up fee of £100 and then monthly rental of £18 (so more expensive than WorldPay).
Transaction costs: 3.99% for credit cards (which for us means 28p per book) and 38.5p for debit cards.

I did have what I thought was a brainwave. Why not put all our offline transactions through WorldPay? That way, we'd only have to pay for one system, and we'd simply go online to process all credit and debit cards. We were delighted with this notion, and called Guy at Pedalo to find out if it could be done. He told us that it's perfectly possible technically, but for legal reasons you have to tell all your offline customers that you're doing it. We don't, unfortunately, think this is a good idea – far too many of them would be unwilling to have us process their cards online. And anyway, without the HSBC machine, what would we do if they declined?

14 January

Rich has had a meeting with Allan Lovegrove at Alton Logistics, thrashing out this issue of discounts among other things. The final decision is 25% for single copies of a book and 35% for more than one. Nice and simple (after all the fuss...). There will, however, be some organisations who simply won't play ball, such as the wholesalers for whom we'll follow Mark's advice and let them beat us down from 40% to 45%. Another exception is the library service who seem to have agreed an across the board discount in the industry of 47% (not that I remember agreeing to that).

Allan will handle all sales within the book trade at 15% plus carriage, which should average 66p per book. So for books we sell at a 35% discount, less Allan's cut and the postage, we'll make a gross profit of (very roughly) £1.94 per book.

We'll be allocated an account manager at Alton Logistics, and we'll get monthly statements which tell us:

- How many books have been sold
- To whom
- The value of the books sold
- Stock levels
- Anything else we ask them to tell us

They'll do all the invoicing and collect all the money, and pay us a month in arrears. Allan advises us not to charge p&p for books we send out from home (which we weren't going to anyway) but says we *should* charge for postage to overseas addresses and Eire as this is expensive.

15 January

Susan Hill called me this morning to say she'd got the book and she thought it looked great. She was altogether extremely positive and encouraging about it. She also gave me the names of a couple of useful journalists, and answered several questions. For example, this reader offer *She* magazine are running in March. I had no idea what level of response to expect. Five orders? 50? She tells me 50 would be good; the best she's ever got is 120.

17 January

Well, there's been lots of activity on the sales and PR front, with quite a few magazines asking for copies of the book. Some of the children's mail order companies Rich has been approaching are also asking to see the book with a view to adding it to their catalogue. It's a slowish process, of course. First we mail or email everyone with the basic information or press release (the books cost us £1 each so we can't afford to send them out to 150 people on the off chance). Next, we call a few days later to see if they are interested in using it. Then we can send them the book, or anything else they say they need, such as a photo of the cover or the author (that's me, folks).

I have discovered a great way to get editorial coverage. Freelance journalists. Actually, this should have been obvious, but I've only just registered the value of it. Freelance journalists get paid to come up with ideas for articles and then write them. So if I can feed them a good idea, such as using management techniques to bring up children, they can make money out of selling an article on the subject which promotes our book. Everyone's happy. And, of course, they have really good contacts in the media which I don't so they're far more likely to get the article placed than I would be.

Unfortunately, I don't know enough freelance journalists. But our old mate Rose Rouse has already got the Sunday Express magazine interested. And I know two or three other journalists whom I've spoken to and who are interested in trying to sell a piece, too – one of them has particularly good contacts among the parenting media. Actually, one of my business publishers put a freelance journalist on to me the other day for a business article she was writing. After I'd given her what she wanted, I switched to my White Ladder hat and told her about *Kids & Co*. She was very interested and wanted to see a copy of the book.

PRESS INFORMATION

I've been sending out an information sheet to the press telling them more about the book, in the hope it will catch their imagination enough to review the book or write a feature around it. This is slightly different from a press release, in that it doesn't present it as a news story (*White Ladder have announced the publication of a new book...*) but gives the editor information about the 'story' within the book.

A few days after this has reached them, I phone them to prompt them. Ostensibly I'm calling to see if they want any more material, and indeed that is a genuine reason for calling. But it's not the only reason. Some editors are never going to use the piece. Some were going to use it before I called. But there is a group in the middle who are more likely to use it if they are reminded that it's there, or who had some vague nagging doubt or question that they can put to me if I'm actually on the end of the phone. Hence there's no point being pushy – just helpful.

It's interesting to look at statistics for responses to mailings (which is essentially what a press release of any kind is). The statistics are for average mailings of any kind so they won't be gospel accurate for any one industry or type of mailing, but

TIME ELAPSED 7 months 2 weeks 3 days

they still give a clear message:

Type of contact	Average response rate
Mail only	2%
Phone only	2–10%
Mail then phone	2–15%
Phone then mail	5–15%
Phone then mail then phone	10–20%

(with thanks to the Calcom Group)

In fact, phone first, then send the information, then phone again is what we have done with the most promising prospects, since Anne (our new agent) phoned round the key parenting publications in early December.

Here's a copy of the information I'm sending out. It should catch an editor's eye easily if it's the kind of thing they'd be likely to want to use, and it should then give them enough information to make a decision on whether to run a story or a review.

KIDS&Co

Winning business tactics for every family

"Ros Jay has had a brilliant idea, and what is more she has executed it brilliantly. KIDS & CO is the essential handbook for any manager about to commit the act of parenthood, and a thoroughly entertaining read for everyone else."

JOHN CLEESE

Most of us spend several years working before becoming parents, and the majority of us continue to work once we have children. At work, you learn all sorts of valuable skills – managing, selling, negotiating and so on – which you can apply in any company you work for. But when you become a parent, all those hard-learned skills are useless. Or are they?

KIDS & Co explains how your business skills don't have to go out of the window when you walk in through the front door. You may sometimes feel that the kids get the better of you every time, but here is one weapon you have that they don't: all those business skills you are familiar with and they know nothing about. Closing the sale, win/win negotiating, motivational skills, and all the rest of them. All you need to do is learn how to apply them to your children as well as to your customers and your staff.

Obviously there is no perfect way to handle our kids so that we never hear a single whinge or tantrum (more's the pity) but there are certainly techniques which make life a whole lot easier. What's more, as we know from our business experience, these techniques work on grown-ups. So they should be effective with children right through to adulthood even when, like customers and staff, they have got wise to the techniques and know what you're up to.

KIDS & Co covers a serious subject – the business of parenting – with a light-hearted touch.

Chapters

1   Customer relations skills: make your children feel they matter
2   Selling skills: get your children to do whatever you want… willingly
3   Negotiating skills: meet each other half way
4   Motivation skills: generate enthusiasm in your children
5   Management skills: get the best from your kids
6   Teamwork skills: show your children how to get along together

Author biography
Ros Jay is a professional author who writes books on both business and

parenting topics, in this case simultaneously. Her books include Fast Thinking Manager's Manual, Build a Great Team and How to Manage Your Boss, all for Prentice Hall, Smart Things to Know about Customers for Capstone, and Baby Sanctuary for Chrysalis Books. She is the mother of three young children and stepmother to another three grown-up ones.

Kids & Co Background information

ISBN: 0 9543914 0 3

New paperback

Publication date: 15 March

Author: Ros Jay

Price: £6.99

Binding: paperback   No of pages: 128   Trim size: 216mm x 138mm

KIDS & Co can be ordered via:

White Ladder Press Ltd

Great Ambrook, Near Ipplepen, Devon TQ12 5UL

Phone 01803 813343

Fax 01803 813928

Email enquiries@whiteladderpress.com

GOLDEN RULE: *Contact journalists by phone as well as in writing.*

Elie Ball, the sales and marketing guru on our editorial board, is coming to stay this weekend. Apart from socialising she's also going to give me and Rich sales and PR masterclasses in the evenings, after the kids have gone to bed. So as from next week we should know twice what we know now about the subject. I've worked in PR before, but

I have nothing like Elie's experience and – crucially – she knows about PR in the publishing world, whereas my experience is more general.

We've had emails back and forth with Guy at Pedalo about finalising the content for the website and giving the final go-ahead. It's all very exciting – I can't wait to see it. The deadline for completion is 24th February.

18 January

We're going on holiday for a week in April. We decided last summer when we were first planning White Ladder that we couldn't give up going on holiday until we can afford a secretary or assistant to cover for us. We have three children aged from 6 downwards, and the idea of telling them that all holidays are cancelled for the next couple of years is unthinkable. But what do we do about the business?

For a start, we can plan publication dates to be well clear of holidays (and have done). But even so, we can't leave the answerphone on for a week with no one fielding calls. It's equally impossible to divert the phones to mobiles. Technically it can be done, but imagine trying to cope with small tired children having tantrums on rainy Cornish beaches and then having the phone ring with someone wanting to place an order ("Could you hold for a moment while I find a pen?").

Anyway, we had a good phone call today from our friends Alastair and Cheryl. They live in Spain and will be over in April but need somewhere to stay. Bingo! They can have our house for nothing if they'll answer our phone. They're both extremely competent and personable, so we have no qualms about letting them loose on our valuable customers.

20 January

Elie has just been down for the weekend. As well as having a great time seeing her, she was also incredibly helpful too. She advised me to get cracking now on all the PR (we're 7 weeks from publication) apart from the daily press, TV and radio (leave them for a couple of weeks).

We talked a lot about selling *Kids & Co* to large organisations who want to present a parent-friendly image to their employees. If you have an image of being encouraging to parents you'll recruit and retain better staff, so anything from flexi-working to company crêches is popular with the personnel departments of many companies (now apparently known as 'People and Change' departments). We think these companies could buy copies of *Kids & Co* and give one to each employee – male or female – who has a baby. It's cheaper than a bunch of flowers, lasts longer and is more useful. What's more, it is relevant to the relationship they have with the person since it relates to work as well as children. And heck, if they're feeling generous they can even give them flowers too.

GOLDEN RULE: *Think creatively about who your customers might be.*

HOW TO WRITE A PRESS RELEASE

Most people who have never written a press release before are understandably very nervous at the prospect. But it's very easy once you know how, and well worth it. Press coverage can do wonders for your business.

In White Ladder's line of work, national press coverage is essential. However, even a business serving only its local community can pull in a lot of enquiries and orders by getting coverage in the local and regional press. If you're selling to other businesses, trade publications are a great publicity vehicle. If you want to know how to contact them, either use a media guide at your local main library or just buy the papers you want to appear in and find their contact details inside.

On average, editors throw away four out of five press releases. They are most likely to use yours if:

- It is interesting to their readers (the key factor)
- It is well and clearly written so it needs a minimum of effort rewriting it

So pick your stories well, send them to the right publications, and write them well and they're much more likely to get printed.

The headline

Any decent editor will rewrite this so that they don't duplicate the headline in the next paper that runs your story. So the purpose of the headline is not to attract the reader's eye, but simply the editor's. And you've got to grab their attention, or your release with end up in the bin with the rest of those 80%. So the two things to achieve with your headline are:

- Make it clear what the story is
- Make it seem interesting enough to appeal to their readers

To do this you need to be punchy (no more than about ten words at the most), and don't try to be clever. Just tell it like it is, and make it sound interesting. For example, *How going to work can make you a better parent*. That sounds intriguing and describes exactly what *Kids & Co* is about.

The first paragraph

If your headline was catchy and interesting enough, the editor will glance at the first paragraph. By the time they get to the end of this, they will probably have decided whether or not to run the story. So what goes into the first paragraph?

- Lead in with the punchline (much as this goes against the grain if you're a natural storyteller). So you might start by saying *White Ladder have announced the publication of a new book* and then going on to give a brief summary of it.
- The alternative, where it is interesting and relative, is to kick off with some kind of little-known fact or statistic. For example *Two thirds of all mothers work...*
- Now give the bare facts – don't worry about details at this stage. So: *Kids & Co is all about how working parents can use their sales and management skills to bring up their children. No more need to feel guilty about going out to work: it's all good training for when you get home.*
- Keep this paragraph brief – no more than around 50 words.
- Press releases are always written in the third person: *White Ladder has announced* not *We have announced*.

The contents

The main thing you need to know is that most ed
they cut a press release, cut it from the bottom up.
ther towards the end something is, the more likely
cut.

- Put important information near the top of the press release.
- Fill in the basic facts, clearly and simply (no fancy jargon or unnecessary long words).
- You're not writing an ad, so don't talk about *an incredible new product*. Just be factual. Answer the questions who, what, when, why, where and how (in our case just a matter of explaining that White Ladder is publishing a new book called *Kids & Co*, on 15 March, and why we think parents need such a book).
- It's a good idea to add a quote or two at the end. It adds a human dimension. You can always quote yourself, as in *publisher Roni Jay said, "We're very excited about this book. We've had a terrific response from the press and it looks set to sell really well"*. Or you can quote a customer, a supplier or anyone else relevant. The easiest approach is to write the quote yourself and then ask them to approve it. So you might say, quoting the endorsement on the book jacket, *According to John Cleese, "Ros Jay has had a brilliant idea, and what is more she has executed it brilliantly. Kids & Co is the essential handbook for any manager about to commit the act of parenthood, and a thoroughly entertaining read for everyone else."*

The layout

This is very straightforward, but best to know the standard format. You can use headed notepaper, or put together a variation on it for press releases, for example with just your logo at the top.

- Head the page PRESS RELEASE.
- Under this put the date of the release, and the words *for immediate release*. The alternative to this phrase, which you're unlikely to need, is *embargoed until...(time and date)*. You only need to embargo a press release if the press need advance warning of something you want kept secret. It's used for things like the New Year's honours lists and celebrity kiss-and-tell memoirs. The press do generally respect embargoes, but they don't appreciate unnecessary ones.
- Try to keep your press release to one side of A4 paper, double spaced. If you have to go on longer than this, write more at the bottom of the page, and then continue on a fresh sheet, not on the back of the first page. Identify the second page in case the two become separated.
- On the line below the end of the material you want printed, put END.
- Then put the date.
- Then give contact details for editors to call you for further information. It helps to give an out of hours number/mobile number too.

27 January

We're both thoroughly enjoying work at the moment – except when we have to stop doing White Ladder work and go back to writing books for other people. Actually, Rich is writing *The Voice of Tobacco* at the moment, which is looking great and which he's really enjoying. He has a proper contract with White Ladder, and he's going to deliver the book on time. We feel it's very important to be professional even though it's just us, and we know we don't really need the manuscript for another couple of months. If we think 'This book's only for White Ladder; it doesn't matter if it's late,' we set a terrible precedent for the future.

Anyway. I've sent out about forty press releases over the last week, to all the publications I'd selected apart from the national daily press, regional and local press, and broadcast media. I shall start chasing them up later this week. Three of them have already been on the phone though asking for review copies of the book.

And hurray! Junior magazine have asked me to write a 2,000 word article based on the book. They'll plug the book at the end, and I'm trying to persuade them to do a reader offer as well. Not something they generally do, but I'm suggesting a format that doesn't involve them in the offer, so maybe they'll go for it. (They just tell readers to phone our number and quote 'Junior offer' if they want to order the book at £1 off the usual price.) The article is going in their April issue, which comes out in March.

Rich spoke this morning to *The Bookseller*, which is *the* trade publication for both publishers and booksellers. He only rang to tell them who our distributor is because that's how it is officially announced to the trade – through *The Bookseller* – but he got chatting to the chap there, who thought White Ladder would make an interesting story for the magazine. This is great news for us. I'd been planning to contact them in a couple of weeks anyway, but we weren't convinced we'd persuade them to give us any coverage. As it is, the chap is certainly going to write a small news piece, but is talking to his editor about doing a news feature on us.

Rich is still getting a good reaction approaching the likes of Mothercare and so on, most of whom he's going to have to wait a couple of weeks at least to get any firm responses out of. One of the catalogues, who seemed very keen and are putting the book forward for selection, told him that the two things which clinched it for them were the endorsement from John Cleese and the photo of Jack on the cover.

DATA PROTECTION EXEMPTION

Rich has just discovered that we don't need to register under the Data Protection Act because we won't be passing our customers' details on to anyone else. You're allowed to keep data without notifying the Data Protection Registrar, apparently, so long as it is only used for:

- Staff administration
- Advertising, marketing and public relations
- Accounts and records

You can get full details about this, to be sure you're exempt, from the Data Protection Registrar or at **www.dpr.gov.uk**

28 January

Rich is getting fed up because the credit card swipe machine hasn't turned up, after his long session with the man from HSBC. Rich can't call him because HSBC have a central number and won't put you through to the branch. They pass on messages – it seems to be all they can do – but no one calls back and Rich just has to leave another message.

WorldPay needed us to get verification from the bank that we are who we say we are. This means turning up at the bank and getting them to look at a passport and then sign a form for WorldPay. Rich wanted to arrange a meeting with the bank, but needed to speak to the branch. To avoid the leave a message/ no one replies scenario, he resolved to get put through to the branch no matter what. He phoned the call centre and asked to be put through.

The woman at the other end said, "Can you tell me what it's concerning?"
Rich was firm and said, "I really need to talk to the branch. Can you put me through please?"
She said, "Please tell me what it's about and I'll see if I can help you."
Rich: "No, you won't be able to. Please put me through."
She (a little more curtly): "Please tell me what you want."
Rich: "I want to speak to my branch."
She, more insistently: "Tell me what it's about. I may be able to help you."
Rich replied with a sigh, "All right, then. When I paid my cheque in this morning, did I leave my glasses on the counter?"
After a pause she replied, "I'll put you through to the branch."
That's a trick worth remembering.

TIME ELAPSED 7 months 4 weeks 0 days

29 January

I spoke to an incredibly helpful journalist at Management Today, who also happens to be a friend of Elie's. She's not sure if she'll be able to review *Kids & Co*, but she may do. In any case, she gave me plenty of useful leads. She also asked what other titles we were planning and when I mentioned this book, *Climbing the Ladder*, she was extremely interested. She says she's been looking for ages for a really good first hand account of starting a small business – there's nothing else like it out there and she thinks it should do well. I hope she's right.

Rachael has recommended an author to us for another title we want to publish next year – got to keep working ahead. It would be very easy to focus fully on *Kids & Co* and fail to keep on top of our future projects. We want to do a book about how to cope with an ailing parent who needs regular or even full time care. We're thinking of calling it *What Shall We Do With Mother?* This was actually an idea of Maggie's (our friend whom we hope will be able to sell *Kids & Co* into corporates). The idea is to do it as a diary; this means we can get humour into it without being offensive, and can have a personal angle that readers can empathise with. A good writer will be able to bring in other strands than their own experience to make it relevant to all sorts of readers, whatever their particular problem.

Anyway, we'd told Rachael about this idea and asked her to keep an eye out for a writer. It really needs to be written genuinely by someone who's been there/is going through it at the moment, which means that we simply can't do it until we have a writer. Rach found out by chance the other day that one of her authors at Pearson Education is currently going through just this scenario with his mother, and might be interested. So I'm going to be talking to him on Friday. Fingers crossed.

> **GOLDEN RULE:** *Look ahead.* You have to juggle your current demands with the future demands of the business. If you focus entirely on the present, in a few weeks or months you'll suddenly find your business starting to fail.

30 January

All this phoning round magazines and newspapers is a long process. Their coverage may be vital to White Ladder but to them, of course, mine is just one more in a pile of press releases on their desk. I'm actually getting a good deal of interest, but no one makes snap decisions about these things. I've been asked to send out about 20 copies of the book, and lots of people are interested in doing articles or reviews. They just haven't confirmed yet.

I have had a few brusque people on the phone, but the vast majority of them are friendly and pleasant even when they're saying no. Consequently I haven't felt demoralised or rejected by the turndowns. I did have one conversation with a columnist from a national newspaper of whom lots of people had said, "Call her, she'll be interested." In fact she was so dismissive it did leave me feeling slightly uncomfortable. But she's been the only one.

I simply don't have time to call all the 180ish people I've mailed. I'm probably going to call around 80 to 100 by the time I've finished. I

122

The White Ladder Diaries

122

The White Ladder Diaries

have a note of the distribution of each publication, and who its readers are. I balance these up to decide which are the most important
ones to call. As a rule of thumb, I call any publication with a distribution over about 75-100,000. But I'll call smaller ones if the readership is well enough targeted. If it's aimed specifically at working parents who have at least some disposable income (to buy books with)
I'd contact a publication quite a lot smaller than that.

31 January

Mark Allin has very kindly sent me a copy of one of Capstone's
books, called *Anyone Can Do It*. It's written by the brother and sister
team who started Coffee Republic, and it's a guide to starting a business, based on their own story. Their start-up costs were around
£90,000 so they had to find funding, and they were looking to building a large chain with a strong brand right from the start. So the
book is slightly geared towards a bigger operation than White Ladder
is – at least at present. It's also slightly slanted towards their own
experience of launching an innovative idea – they were the first to
bring US-style coffee bars to the UK – rather than starting the kind of
business which already exists. We hope we've found a market niche
with White Ladder, but the idea of selling books is hardly a new one
to spring on the public.

Nevertheless, there's a mass of stuff in *Anyone Can Do It* which is very
relevant to us, and their story is a fascinating one, even though we
all know the ending before we begin: that Coffee Republic grows to
be a highly successful business. I was reassured and encouraged to
find that their early experiences – the stuff we've covered already like

preliminary market research and the business plan – were very similar to ours, and they learnt much the same lessons as we have.

If you're serious about starting a business, whatever size, I certainly recommend reading *Anyone Can Do It – Building Coffee Republic From Our Kitchen Table: 57 Real-life Laws on Entrepreneurship* by Sahar and Bobby Hashemi, published by Capstone.

GOLDEN RULE: *Read everything relevant you can get your hands on.* All my reading at the moment is White Ladder related – books, articles and magazines about publishing, marketing and setting up a business.

It's been a good start to the day. First a phone call from Woman magazine to ask for a copy of *Kids & Co* (I sent them a press release), and then an email from the features editor at The Independent, whom I spoke to yesterday and then emailed, asking for a copy of the book too. It will be next week at least before I find out if either of them actually decides to run a piece about it, but it's extremely encouraging just to get this much response.

Rich and I have been questioning our decision not to grow bigger than ten titles a year. Assuming we get far enough to have the choice (and we're increasingly optimistic that we will) we feel that a business, like a plant, needs to grow if it is to survive. A publishing business isn't generally destined to grow into a multi-national conglomerate so we'd never be talking massive growth. We're wondering why we need to stop at ten titles a year. Better to decide that we'll keep growing so long as we can do it without compromising our basic premise that we give every book individual marketing time and attention. So long as it's cost effective to employ the staff we need to do that, there's no reason why we shouldn't publish thirty, forty, fifty books a year or more.

We've also been talking about branding. Most people advise us – and we ourselves have been thinking – that since most readers haven't a clue who publishes the books they read (I include myself in this) we should focus on promoting the individual titles rather than the White Ladder brand. The brand is only really relevant for selling to the retailers (both in and out of the book trade).

However, one person has been telling us that we should pay more attention to branding. And that one person is Mark Allin. Now, if it were almost anyone else I would probably disregard it. But I have enormous respect for Mark's opinion on this kind of thing, and certainly Capstone have a stunningly strong brand image which they are known for. So I've been thinking about it. And the more I think about it, the more sure I become that Mark is right. We really need the booksellers – along with mail order catalogues and all the other outlets – to notice our books and think, "If it's a White Ladder book, we'll order a few copies. They always get great publicity and their books always sell."

But how do we promote our brand effectively with only one title and no advertising budget? I'm going to have to ask Mark about this. I'll give him a ring.

1 February

I spoke to the author Rachael put me on to yesterday, and with any luck we have an author for *What Shall We Do With Mother?* He's a professional writer – I've had a look at his stuff and it's very good – and he has a mother who is in Scotland (he's in the home counties) and who is, sadly, in what he and his family believe is the early stages of Alzheimer's. He seems to understand and appreciate exactly what we're after, and he has the humour to do the book; he agrees that humour is essential. He's even been keeping notes of his experiences with his mother's illness because he finds it cathartic to keep writing it down.

Obviously, however, it would be a very emotional process for him (we'd realised this would be the case with any author we found). He feels this might be a positive process for him, but equally it may not. He also needs to consider how his family would feel about him putting his mother's experiences into a book. So he's going to think about it and get back to us when he's reached a decision. Can't say fairer than that.

I spoke to the chap at *The Bookseller* again yesterday – he interviewed me about both White Ladder generally and *Kids & Co* specifically. He asked me some fairly astute questions about how we were planning to promote *Kids & Co*, and how we expected to keep it selling after the initial publicity campaign. I think I managed to answer his questions in a way which sounded as though we knew what we were doing – they are all questions we've thought about ourselves and actually we do know what we're doing. We may not know if it's the *right* thing to be doing, but we do know what it is.

TIME ELAPSED   8 months   0 weeks   1 days

Anyway, *The Bookseller* isn't in the business of writing damaging articles about small publishers. If they thought we were a bunch of losers they simply wouldn't run the piece at all. They may express the odd reservation (although I hope not) but they won't do a hatchet job. In fact, though, with my less neurotic hat on (I rather like that image) I think I probably did fine. He's going to let us know when they'll run the piece.

3 February

I had an email from Mark this morning in reply to mine asking if he could talk to me about branding:

> I do have some strong views on the value of brand development. It certainly served Capstone well. It's not a question of whether readers recognise the brand of the publisher. If publishers don't promote their brand values then of course no-one cares. But what about Dorling Kindersley, Penguin, Picador, Virago, Walker Books etc? They all care(d) about communicating with customers, about creating a shared set of values between the reader and publisher. With one book of course there is a limited amount you can do but no harm in starting with promotion in the books, building mailing lists, website etc
>
> I am here all morning so give me a call.

I called him, and had a very useful conversation. He emphasised that a lot of the reason that readers don't know who publishes the books they read is because the publishers don't bother to make it clear. In fact, Mark believes, if you make your brand strong enough, readers *will* be aware of it. Capstone became noticed for being rebellious, cutting edge, radical among business publishers from the start. They created this image through everything they did, from their choice of subject matter, the style of the writing, the design of the book covers, their catalogues, even the fact that they put their logo at the top of the spine on their books (it traditionally goes at the bottom).

If you have a really clear image of your brand in your own mind, and consciously follow it through in everything you do, you will be promoting it without having to spend any money on it (which of course we haven't got). As time goes on you can then spend money when you have it, and you'll be reinforcing an already established brand. Even if you don't spend money directly on it, you'll strengthen it as you spend money on promotional material, product design and so on. If you don't do this, you may unwittingly project the wrong image at the start, and have to undo all that work before you start to build a brand image later. Capstone didn't have a masterplan. They simply had a clear vision and made sure they imparted it in everything they did.

This is encouraging, because I think we're doing this already. But talking to Mark focused me far more on making sure that the White Ladder brand comes across strongly on everything from press releases (worth establishing a clear image early on with journalists) to business cards. He feels that our 'new tricks for old dogs' is a great strapline for making us very aware of exactly what image we want to promote. In our case, because we want to sell direct to customers and eventually bring out a mail order catalogue, having a recognisable brand is going to be even more important.

> **GOLDEN RULE:** *Get everything right from the start.* Even when it hardly shows – from branding to databases to your website – you can start small, but you must be on the right road from the outset.

> **GOLDEN RULE:** *Look after the details.* A brand is largely built on detail – as is good customer service, a high quality product and all the other things that matter.

Great phone call with the editor of *Executive Woman* magazine. I called and asked if she'd got the press release I sent her. No, she hadn't seen it. So I told her, "The book's about using sales and management techniques to bring up your children." She replied, "Great! I love it! Right, I'll have a 650 word article in the next three weeks and I'm running it in the May issue. And send me a jpeg of the cover." No messing – straight to the point. Wonderfully refreshing.

4 February

Had a call from the editor of *Personal & Finance Confidential* this morning. She wants a 700 word article for their March issue, and she's going to run a short review of the book with a reader offer. We send a free copy to the first three people to send in the coupon, and we get the names and addresses of all the respondents.

The parenting editor of *The Times* also wants a copy of the book.

The PR is obviously paying off, although I still feel I'm wasting quite a bit of time only I don't know which bit. It's worth spending hours chasing some leads, while others probably don't warrant more than five minutes. Some are worth mailshotting and that's it – either they go for it or they don't. Overall I'm happy to put in a solid month of PR, so long as I get a good return for it. But on future titles I'm going to have to learn where to invest the time and where to let it go.

Ned's old nursery teacher, Jill, came round today. She left teaching to go back to hairdressing, which she does in people's homes, and she came to cut the boys' hair. Rich showed her a copy of *Kids & Co*, and she reckoned she could sell it to various other parents she visits. So he gave her a copy, and a handful of flyers which he marked with her initials. He agreed that if we get any orders back on her flyers, we give her £2 commission.

5 February

Following on from talking to Mark about branding, I've been investigating the cost of getting bookmarks printed. Ideally we should print these as offcuts of book covers (to save money on printing), but since we're not printing book covers at the moment it may be worth doing them on their own for now. Then we can think about getting future reprints done at the same time as covers.

We're thinking of having our white ladder on a blue background – our logo on our book spines in other words – with a dog climbing up it. Under that would be our logo, including the strapline 'new tricks for old dogs'. Below that simply our phone number and website address. It looks like thousand would cost us around £150 to print, but adding extra thousands (run-ons as printers call them) would only cost an additional £31 per thousand run-on. We'll have to add design costs on to that, but I think they should be very small on top of what we'll be doing for the website anyway. We were already thinking of adding a dog to the ladder for parts of the website.

6 February

Well, Jill didn't hang around. On the school run this morning, Rich saw one of the other parents who handed him an order for *Kids & Co*. Jill evidently cut her children's hair yesterday, and showed her the book. Not only did Holly order a copy, but she also wants to take a handful of flyers with exactly the same deal. Rich and I are now wondering how we can roll this system out on a bigger scale. Who are the best people to approach, and how can we get at them cheaply and effectively?

Just had an email from Rachael Stock. What a star. She's got us an appointment with the head of People and Change at Pearson to talk about them buying *Kids & Co* to give to staff who go on maternity or paternity leave. If we can persuade them to take a few copies, then we can go to other big companies and say, in effect, 'Pearson are doing it. How about you?'

I'm also holding off on sending a press release to all the personnel journals and magazines, because the story I want them to cover is that a big corporate (maybe Pearson, with luck) has bought copies of this new business-related childcare book...

I've been contacting the national press over the last week or so. I've

posted some press releases and emailed others, to s[...]
best approach. On balance, email seems to be [...]
Obviously if I phone in advance I ask which they'd [...]
excuse for phoning, apart from anything else. I c[...]
release about the book would interest them, and the [...]
like me to send it.

EMAILING PRESS RELEASES

Newspaper editors are deluged with press releases, both by post and email, so you need to get their attention to read yours. This is why a phone call in advance is often a smart move; it just means they'll recognise the press release when it comes through in the next 24 hours or so. Apart from that, here are a couple more tips:

- Give the email a catchy subject line. For example, for *Kids & Co* I tend to put 'How to bring work home with you' or sometimes 'The perfect work/life balance' (both suggestions courtesy of Elie, I seem to remember). The subject header's purpose is to get them to read the covering letter, so it needs to sound interesting.
- The press release itself goes as an attachment, so you need to add a covering note. This should be as brief as possible as a rule, since everything you have to say should already be in the press release itself. All you're trying to do is get them to open the attachment. I generally put something like, *I'm attaching some information about Kids & Co, a quirky new book about using sales and management techniques to bring up children*. I reckon that if there's any chance they'll be interested, that will persuade them to open the attachment. If it doesn't, they'd never have used the story anyway. After this

brief opener, I simply add a line inviting them to contact me if they want any more info, or a review copy.

- I generally send the same message to a dozen or so editors at once, but I email each one separately (rather than putting, for example, 'undisclosed recipients' at the top). This would be impractical if I were emailing hundreds, but I think the personal touch makes it worthwhile for just a few at a time. I also personalise the start of each email, 'Dear so-and-so'. I use Christian names only on an email, being an informal medium, where I use the full name on a letter.

On a technical note, I am training myself always to insert the attachment before I do anything else, so I can't forget it. This would not only make me look like an inefficient prat, but the odds are they're not going to bother to reply and ask for the attachment. They'll just move on to the next email. It may be one way to get yourself remembered, but it's not a good way.

As a double check, I also put in the address to which I'm sending the email last, and run a quick check that I've done everything else before I key it in. In my case this means:

- Adding the attachment
- Writing the subject line
- Pasting in the email itself and putting their name at the top
- Selecting my sender's address as roni@whiteladderpress.com and not my personal email

I wrote that last entry this morning, since when I've decided email is definitely best. I spoke to someone at the Sunday Times Style magazine earlier who is interested in maybe doing a feature. It's not definite – she has to speak to the relevant editor – but she seems very hopeful. Then I had a call from the editor of the Times Magazine (which comes out on a Saturday). She wants to do a proper feature – interviewer, photographer etc (God, I hate that) – and a reader offer of some kind. But she needs me to agree we won't do any other coverage until afterwards, so she gets to go first. This doesn't mean reviews, but no other features. On the other hand, she's talking about doing a piece on 1 March, so we still have two weeks before publication to get other coverage (the nationals aren't interested once the book's actually published).

I don't imagine she's bothered about coverage in monthly magazines either, such as Junior, but in any case I think they all come out after 1 March. However, we wouldn't be able to do a piece for Style until after that. We reckon that the Times Magazine is probably a better bet than Style, although we'd like both, so if we're lucky enough to have to choose, we'll go for the Magazine. It's a smaller distribution, actually, but probably a higher relevant readership for that section of the paper. What we really want, of course, is for the Magazine to do the piece on 1 March and for Style to run a feature subsequently. Well, nothing's in the bag yet so we're trying not to get too excited until it's definite. (But we're failing. We *are* very excited.)

7 February

Rich had an email yesterday evening from someone at BCA, who own almost all the book clubs. She said that they simply don't consider books that sell at a price as low as £6.99, because they can't discount them enough to be worthwhile. Bugger.

Still, the point of selling through book clubs is not to make a fortune, since the margins are always very tight. It's better to look at it as a form of PR, since it gives your book good exposure. So it's not a great loss, and we're not getting depressed about it. Everything else is going so well we have a real 'don't care' attitude about that sort of thing just at the moment.

11 February

We've seen our website! Guy sent us through its temporary address and it's looking great. A small handful of details to sort out, but it looks clean and smart and it's really fast, which is essential. They'll add a dog (climbing the ladder, probably) in a couple of weeks when the designer's back from holiday, which will give the site a lift visually, but we can get the site up and running before that. It should be live by the end of this week.

The other thing which may take another couple of days to sort out is all the database stuff, enabling us to enter our offline customers' details as well as automatically storing data supplied by our online customers.

We had only two comments of any real significance – more than just spelling mistakes and the like:

- Every time we clicked on the 'go to checkout' button it took us to 'terms and conditions' first. Only after scrolling down through this page and clicking on 'I agree' at the bottom could we proceed to buy the book. We do need customers to agree to our terms and conditions, but I've asked Guy if we could put the 'I agree to the terms and conditions' button on the checkout page itself, and allow people to choose whether they visit the 'terms and conditions' page. Officially of course everyone should read it before agreeing, but we all know that most people click on the button without ever looking at the terms and conditions they're agreeing to. If this amendment is too expensive, our fallback option is to add a line at the top of the terms and conditions page which says, 'Please read through the following terms and conditions, and click on the button at the bottom of the page to proceed to the checkout.

- We wanted to be able to send customers a confirmation of their order. WorldPay confirm the credit card transaction, but not the order itself. Even if we haven't the resources at the moment to specify what the order was, we can at least say, 'Thank you for ordering from White Ladder Press. We've received your order and will despatch it shortly. Please let us know if it hasn't arrived in seven working days.' We'll probably set this up so we have to click one button manually to send it after we've picked up the order. This means if we ever run out of stock we don't automatically send the email, but can send a personal one apologising etc instead.

We've been panicking about what to do if we get loads of phone calls at the beginning of March and can't handle them all. We've no idea what response to expect to the reader offers we've got running in She, Junior, Devon Today and Personal & Finance Confidential, all of which come out in the first week in March (assuming they all agree to run the reader offers). I think if we have loads of calls it will only be for a day or two, but we need to have a contingency plan.

We've registered for BT's Call Minder so we have an answerphone if both our lines are engaged (and we've recorded our own message for it). And if necessary we can transfer calls to another phone too if ours is engaged. So we could find a willing volunteer anywhere in the country to field calls for us for a day or two if necessary.

Rich is also finding out – though I doubt we'll need it this time – how to use call centres, what they cost, what notice they need and so on.

> **GOLDEN RULE:** *Make contingency plans.* You have no idea at this stage what might happen, so think through the worst – or best – scenario and make sure you're prepared for coping with it.

The Times Magazine want me to travel to London with the children so they can photograph us. The children at a board table, backs of their heads only, and me at the other end of the table with a flip chart. So that's about $4^1/_2$ hours each way with a six, a three and a one year old, plus a boring hour or so in the middle being photographed. Sounds like a fun day out, hey?

When I pointed out the drawbacks from my perspective, plus the fact that two of the children are in school anyway, they were actually very understanding. I suggested I try to find someone down here who has a boardroom they can lend us. Or I go up to London on my own (I'm up for the day next week anyway seeing the Director for People at Pearson) – since they're only photographing the backs of the children's heads, I pointed out that they don't really need to use *my* children. Anyone's would do.

We had two orders in the post today, both on flyers we'd put in local shops or Jill had distributed. Looks like Rich's idea could be a success.

I had a call from Matthew Clarke at Torbay Bookshop this morning. He very kindly rang to let me know that he'd had the March catalogue through from Gardners (one of the big wholesalers) and that *Kids & Co* wasn't listed. He also offered to order a couple of copies from each of the two main wholesalers, just to try and kick-start the system. He'll order other copies from us – we can give him a better deal than they will, and we'll still be better off ourselves too.

Matthew's also given me the low-down on the best way to get local press coverage; then he can promote the book in his shop too, and he should sell a good few he reckons.

I've been on to Gardners who say they're only supplying the book to order, not actually carrying it as a stock line (I was a little confused – since they ordered three copies back in November I had assumed they were stocking it). The buyer said he'd see how it sold for a few months before making a decision. If it sells 5-10 copies a month, and keeps that rate up after the initial publication, they might stock it. I offered to send him a copy, mentioned John Cleese's endorsement, and also the articles in *The Bookseller* and *The Times Magazine*, and he softened a little. He said if I sent him a copy he'd think about it again. Can't say fairer than that, so we'll just wait and see what happens...

It occurred to me that this journal has very little to say about selling, since I'm not doing very much of it. So to redress the balance, I asked Rich to write me a few notes summarising what he's been up to over the last few weeks. Here's the email he sent me:

> At the moment I am working on three fronts:
> I am emailing every website, children's catalogue, book club
> etc that comes my way. From these I am getting quite a good
> response. If the email is successful in the sense that they allow
> a telephone approach then I phone. I play the sort of friendly
> incompetent rather than the pushy salesman. I explain that this
> is our first book and I haven't a clue what I am supposed to do
> next. And I politely ask what their procedure is for presenting a
> new product to them. They have all been helpful and under-
> standing and polite in this respect and explained what I am
> supposed to do. I then do this and they can't complain as they
> have told me to do it. 'We usually ask for the book to be sent
> to us for review and then you're supposed to phone us after a
> few days to make sure we've got it. Then you phone again to
> make sure we've read it.'
>
> I've been getting quite a lot of laughs by playing it this way. It
> seems to work and people are basically very nice.
>
> Second front. I am collecting a team of reps by offering people
> the chance to earn £2 per book if they distribute our leaflets.
> They have to mark each leaflet so we know where it came from.
> We have already generated a few sales this way and we've only
> just begun this approach. I like it. I envision a whole team of
> people out there selling on our behalf. A dedicated, loyal team
> of leaflet distributors. At £2 per book it works out at about
> 28.5% which is a damn sight better than we get from anyone
> else – Amazon 60%, wholesale distributors such as Gardners
> 45%. It means we still make just over £4 profit per book after
> printing costs. I am also looking into distributing leaflets by just

getting them into shops, cafes, etc. There is of course no discount to pay by this method and we collect all the profit. We have had one order from this already and we only started it a couple of days ago.

Third front is to persuade organisations such as schools to include a leaflet with their regular mailings. We have offered the same £2 discount but presented it as fundraising for the school. Our first mailing should go out from St Christopher's in a week or two. It will be interesting to see what response we get.

Selling doesn't seem to be such a nightmare as I had thought it was going to be. Mark Allin's comment that 'you are not selling, you are offering them a partnership' has worked extremely well and I don't think of myself as a slippery salesman but rather a buddy, a chum, offering these people the chance to participate in our profitable business.

Talking to people on the phone is OK as well. I thought it would be daunting to do this 'cold calling' bit but instead if you phone them up and ask their advice – 'We have published this book and were wondering how to get you to read it' sort of approach – it seems to pay off.

I'm now beginning to feel very confident that I can achieve some sales; these sales might not be extraordinary but they will be sales and a month or two ago I wasn't certain I could sell anything to anyone.

Relative costs/profits

Getting the book logged onto amazon.co.uk is proving problematic. It is a very roundabout method involving sending a

picture of the cover via FTP files – they won't accept emailed pictures. Plus you have to follow their guidelines exactly to the letter or your submission gets rejected – this isn't guidelines this is rules and regulations. Plus they take a 60% discount – wow! This is more than anyone else. From our £6.99 a title they take £4.19 leaving us a mere £2.80, out of which we have to pay our distributor 15% so that's another 42p gone – and Amazon won't take your book unless you distribute it through a distributor with whom they already have an account. This leaves us £2.38. As it costs us around £1 a book the profit on this is £1.38. Take out royalties of 30% – 84p – we actually make 54p a book if we sell through Amazon.

If we sell a book ourselves via a leaflet or the phone it costs us only the postage of 72p – profit is thus £6.27. Take off royalties of 30% (£2.10) and printing (£1); we get a profit of £3.17. That's better.

Finally, if we sell to bookshops we'll incur a discount of 45% thus our £6.99 brings us in £3.84. Deduct Alton Logistic's 15% (58p), the 30% royalty (£1.15) and the printer's £1 that leaves £1.11 profit to White Ladder. By golly we have to sell a lot of books to make this profitable.

It does give you a thrill though to bank cheques even if it is only 2 for £6.99 each at the moment. But from this tiny start we shall grow and grow.

GOLDEN RULE: *You're not selling, you're offering a partnership.* If you find the prospect of hard selling daunting, remind yourself you're simply offering people a deal which will benefit them as well as you.

13 February

Rich had a complete genius of an idea last night. At least, I think so. We'd been wondering how to recruit people like Jill and Holly all over the country to sell books for us. Every order we get in with their name on the order form, we pay them £2. Well, I think Rich has just cracked it.

It's so simple. We put a flyer in with every book we send out inviting people to contact us if they'd like to earn some money selling our books. Part of the joy of this is that we're approaching people who have already bought the book, so they have a ready 'display copy' if they want it. I didn't want to ask people to sell without seeing the book, but we couldn't very well give away free copies to anyone who claimed they were going to sell for us and then didn't. We could ask people to buy the book if they want to sell it on, but that smacks of those dodgy schemes in the small ads where you have to invest money before you see anything back. Rich's idea solves all these problems, and gives us the perfect way to find sales people.

I can see this being a really successful, and innovative, way to sell books. And I love the idea of running a freelance sales force. Rich can handle all the admin and finance side of it – he says that's very straightforward. We'd probably pay everyone their accumulated £2s once a month, otherwise we'd be issuing endless cheques for £2.

What *I'd* enjoy doing is finding ways to motivate the sellers and help them sell more books for their benefit as well as ours. We could send out a small booklet giving advice and ideas on how to distribute leaflets – to shops and so on – and how to use them to raise funds for a charity or a local school. And I'm full of ideas for giving them a newsletter (including an exchange of ideas between them), rewarding them every time they hit 20 sales or whatever, giving a prize to the person who's sold the most books each month and so on.

We're trying not to get excited, but we think this could be a big success. I'm getting a quote from the printer for 1,000 leaflets inviting people to become White Ladder reps (we want to find a better term for them). Then we can start straight away and see if it works or not. And it will hardly cost us anything.

And as if we could stand any more excitement... Guy has sorted out all the minor glitches etc on the website, and this morning had the admin section of it ready for us to look at. This is the private section which we use to access the database. All details, orders etc which website customers enter are tracked here, and we can also put in our own data which we collect offline.

Pedalo have done such a good job. It looks great and it's really easy to use. We can record everything we wanted to, send email confirmations of orders, add notes on customers, do mass emailings and so on. There are one or two things we can't do...yet. That's because our budget has run out. But we can add them as soon as we have the money. The two main things I think we'll be adding fairly soon are:

- Customer search. At the moment customers are listed in the order they register. While there are only a few this really isn't a problem, but if we build up hundreds it will be. When that time comes Pedalo can add a search facility of some kind for us.
- Selected emailings. We can choose who we do and don't send a particular email to already, but we have to go into each individual customer's entry and click or unclick on a box. Again, it's fine with a few customers, but prohibitively time-consuming with a lot of

them. Guy says this is easy to refine so that we sim
whatever fields we want to select. But of course it takes
is money, so that can wait too.

Quite honestly, I still can't believe what we've got for under £4,000
(plus VAT, which we claim back anyway). Some businesses pay tens
of thousands and upwards for databases with less capability and a
less user-friendly website.

> If you want a low budget, high performance website, I can
> thoroughly recommend Pedalo.
> Check them out at **www.pedalo.co.uk**

17 February

Rich is being driven slowly mad by the bank. Actually, not that slowly. Having been promised our swipe machine for tomorrow (only
after making a huge fuss) he'd heard nothing. We've now finally got
hold of our bank manager's direct line, so Rich called them and they
put Rich in touch with the swipe machine people. When Rich spoke
to them about arrangements for the machine coming tomorrow,
they actually laughed at him, and said, "Tomorrow? Who told you
that?" Rich told him that if he was running a business and a customer was this unhappy with a product that hadn't turned up, he'd
put it in the boot of his own car and drive it straight over to the customer. The bloke on the other end of the phone at HSBC said, "If I
did that, I'd spend my entire life in the car driving all over the country."

It turns out that the forms Rich filled out on 15 January only arrived the relevant department two days ago, which is why they haven't got the machine to us already.

Anyway, after a whole morning on the phone, Rich has now got them to say that they guarantee the machine will arrive next Tuesday. We have orders trickling in already, and it's just luck no one has ordered by credit card yet. Anyway, Rich asked them to put their guarantee in writing, but they refused. Our bank manager, however, is on the case, and we hope it really will arrive early next week.

Rich has become so fed up with dealing with HSBC that he contacted Lloyds, thinking we should maybe move our account. However, he couldn't get hold of the right person at Lloyds either, since they too refuse to put you through. They took a message from him at the call centre at Lloyds about ten days ago, and today someone called Rich back. When Rich explained the problem, the chap at Lloyds told him, very frankly, that there was no point moving. "We're all as bad as each other," he said. "We have people leaving us in droves to join HSBC, and the other way around."

Rich asked him why it is impossible to speak to the person you want to any more. The bloke told him, "It's because we were getting so many complaints. Customers were phoning the branches to complain about things, so management's solution was to stop customers talking to anyone but call centre operatives, who can only take messages." Anyway, not only are Lloyds evidently as bad as HSBC – and the other high street banks by all accounts – but they are also more expensive when it comes to swipe machines. So it looks as if we might as well stay with HSBC.

The White Ladder D.

18 February

We've designed a simple leaflet to go out with our books, and we're having 1,000 of them run off. It's cheaper to photocopy than to print, but the quality isn't as good. So we decided to have them printed, but we shopped around for quotes. They're costing us £70, and there's no VAT. The rules for what you do and don't pay VAT on at printers and copy bureaux are extremely complicated, but basically if it's a flyer (like this one) there's no VAT. If it's a letter – of any description – or a form which the recipient is intended to fill in, it's VATable. Anyway, the printers themselves seem to know the system so they can advise.

GETTING QUOTES

It's always worth shopping around for prices because they can vary widely. Three quotes is generally enough to give a clear idea of the range. In this case, we had print quotes for £70 (the one we chose) and also for £109. We had photocopying quotes for £35 and £97.50.

When looking for prices, here are a couple of guidelines:
1   Always make sure you get like-for-like quotes. In our case this meant 100gsm satin art paper, printing in 2 colours (black and our house blue), for 1,000 copies. If you let one printer advise you to use a different paper, for example, and they give you a quote on that basis, you can no longer compare it directly with your other quotes.
2   You can always ask each printer to quote for more than one type of paper, more than one range of colours, more than one quantity and so on.

3 Don't assume the cheapest quote is necessarily the one to choose. Consider the quality – ask to look at samples if necessary. And consider how important quality is to you. For us, it's always important which is why we've chosen to use two colours and a heavyish paper for a flyer. But it is still a flyer so we're not prepared to splash out too much (not on our present budget, anyway).

Here's the text of the flyer we're sending out. This is printed in black with our blue logo above it and a matching blue border around the whole thing.

If you like this book, how about earning a few bob recommending it to other people?

We're looking for people who would like to earn a bit of extra cash, or maybe fundraise for a local school or a favourite charity, by helping to sell *Kids & Co.*

The deal's very simple. If you're interested, we'll send you a handful of leaflets with an order form on the back. All you have to do is to mark them with your name and hand them out. Give them to friends, leave them in shops... we'll give you a few ideas to get you started. No need to do any hard selling if you're not comfortable with that. Then, for every order that comes back with your name on, we pay you a healthy commission. It's as simple as that. When you're ready for more leaflets, we'll send them to you.

If you want to know more, call Richard on 01803 814124. We'd love you to join us.

GOLDEN RULE: *Keep your printing simple.* It's that old 'keep it simple' rule again. If you only pay for something simple, you can afford to do it smartly and well. Don't spend your budget on unnecessary colours or quantities, and then have to economise on quality.

I've just had a phone call from Alan Street, the buyer at Gardners, following my letter to them with a copy of the book. He likes it, and says "It's got a lot of credibility; I've seen a lot worse. And that's a compliment." He drives a hard bargain: 55% and 90 days. I said it wasn't really my department, but we were thinking in terms of 45% and maybe more later if they move enough copies. His best offer then was 55% but direct to us (i.e. no 15% to the distributor) and 30 days, and he'll take 100 copies. I said I was sure we could find a compromise, but he'd have to talk to Rich tomorrow as it's his department, not mine. That buys Rich time to take advice before calling him back.

Anyway, I have to say I was impressed that he was prepared to reconsider, and he's been more willing to go out on a limb than the other wholesalers.

The website went live this afternoon, and we've got our first order through it. It's from our accountant.

20 February

I went up to London to see the Director for People at Pearson plc. What a nice guy. He likes *Kids & Co* (which I'd sent him in advance) and has ordered 10 copies. That's as many as he can use for now at Pearson plc, which only employs 100 people. However, Pearson's three subsidiaries – FT, Penguin and Pearson Education – each have their own heads of HR, who could order (in larger quantities) for their own companies. So David Bell (whom I saw) has invited me to the next heads of HR meeting on 19 March, to try and sell the idea to all of them too.

I had lunch with Rachael beforehand, and we both had ideas spilling out of us as usual when we get together. It was a great couple of hours, and always good to see Rach anyway. She thinks the idea of putting flyers in the books we sell to recruit people to sell for us is simply brilliant.

Meanwhile... back at home, Rich took all the advice he could about Gardners, which amounted to 'Do it their way and, if we get the sales, then we can renegotiate.' So it's 55% and sale or return, but each month's sales will be paid to us 30 days from the end of the month. If it goes well, they'll be prepared to renegotiate in a few months.

Rich and I emailed about 50 people between us from our address books, and asked them to take a look at the website for us. Lots of useful comments have come back, almost all positive, with a few easy to put right glitches. And about 5 orders.

21 February

The Observer might run a piece on *Kids & Co*. It's all getting very exciting.

Our credit card machine finally turned up, two and a half months after Rich started hassling. The bank insist this kind of delay is virtually unheard of – let's hope they're right. Anyway, Rich says it's actually very easy to use because the display tells you exactly what to do.

Rich talked to our distributor about call centres, and it turns out that you can't redirect calls to them if you get swamped. You have to have given out their number in the first place. So that's not an option for us then. Still, we have call minder in place and we have to hope that if we get more calls than we can handle for a week or two, that will cope with the overflow.

I've been getting to grips with the database, entering details of people who have ordered using our order forms. It's very simple once you get used to it, although data entry is inevitably time consuming. We've decided that all order forms go to Rich first. He packs them and then marks the form 'Sent' (or something) so we know the order has gone. It's so easy to put down a pile of orders in the wrong place because you stop to answer a phone or something, and then pick them up later and not be certain whether or not you despatched them. So we hope this system will ensure there's no duplications or missed orders. Then the forms come to me, and I enter the data on to the database.

We figure if we get so many orders that the time involved is excessive, we'll be making enough money to pay someone to come in and do the order fulfilment and data entry for us – even if only part time.

Matthew at the Torbay Bookshop called. He had kindly ordered three copies of *Kids & Co* from Bertrams, one of the big wholesalers, to kick start their ordering system. He was letting us know that Bertrams had given him less than half of their standard discount. If other bookshop owners discover that this is the case, they will only order *Kids & Co* if they have a specific customer order; they won't want to stock it at such a low margin.

The problem, of course, is that our discount to Bertrams is too low at only 35%, and in the long run this is going to do us more harm than good. This is where the whole discount thing gets complicated in ways we hadn't anticipated. We have to give the wholesalers 50-55%, so that they can pass on to the bookshops a discount that gives everyone a workable margin. So Rich is getting on to Bertrams to agree terms which suit everyone.

24 February

Well, Bertrams aren't keen on that idea. They don't want anything to do with us, in fact. They have no interest in stocking *Kids & Co*, which is a real shame. Rich told the buyer all the promotion we have planned, and pointed out that once these various articles are printed, customers may be going into their local shops wanting to order the books, and Bertrams won't be stocking it. Won't they be missing out on business? The buyer told him that was a risk they were prepared to take. I have to say our attitude is, "We'll show 'em." We can stocked the book.

26 February

Anne, our replacement agent, has just left the agency giving us our third agent in four months. During this time, our foreign rights sales have taken a back seat. The replacement agent is now going to have to learn the ropes before anything happens, and we've decided we can't hang around indefinitely. So we're looking for a foreign rights agent to sell the rights for *Kids & Co* and *The Voice of Tobacco*.

We know absolutely nothing about foreign rights agents, so as usual we're asking Mark Allin, Rachael, Susan Hill, Elie and anyone else we can think of. Elie thinks she knows someone good, so we're following that lead up first.

> **GOLDEN RULE:** *Don't be afraid to ask.* You can't possibly know everything. If you're stumped, think who you know who can give you the answer, or at least point you in the right direction, and ask them.

We want to put stickers on all the envelopes we send out with our address on them, in case the books need to be returned by the Post Office. We were looking into the price of having them printed in blue on white, with our logo. But they seem to cost about £60 per thousand. That's about 6p a sticky label. We've decided we can't justify this on our present budget, so we'll have to get ordinary cheapo

labels done instead, with our name and address in plain type. Ah, well.

The Times have moved the feature from 8 March to 15th. However, the Observer are doing a piece this Sunday, I hope. Not a big feature but a nice review leading into a columnists article. The journalist who interviewed me this afternoon for it loved the book, and she has six boys aged between 4 and 17, so I reckon that's a pretty good endorsement.

28 February

The main White Ladder phone line has been down since Tuesday, as has my direct line *and* my modem line. BT routed calls to my personal phone number, but that too was intermittently faulty until this morning, when it became totally dead. The idea is that if you have a business line they 'guarantee' to fix it before the end of the working day after you report it, or they pay you compensation. We don't want compensation, we want a phone. I have had 4 days of rising levels of apoplexy, not helped by BT not having a clue what's happening half the time, and even signing the job off as fixed while two of my lines were still dead.

On Sunday, *The Observer* is running a piece with our phone number at the end of it for people who want to order the book. If there is no phone on Monday morning I will explode with rage and frustration, take myself off to wherever the BT engineers hang out, and personally dismember every one of them. That's unless I accidentally sign the job off as completed when I've only dismembered half of them.

Maggie Tree has come up trumps. I had a long chat with her today (on the only line which was working at the time) and she came up with all sorts of useful things. For example, she's sold to Adams (the kids' clothes chain) in the past and knows who to talk to and how to get in with them. Anyway, she also offered to send out 2,000 flyers for us with her next mailing on Monday – it goes to school teachers – at no cost. In fact, she's even paying the extra few quid the fulfilment house charges for putting an extra leaflet in with the mailing. So 2,000 flyers duly went out in the post this afternoon.

Rich has worked out how to put our A5 flyers through the printer and print a code discreetly in the corner of each one. This means we can track as the orders come in which mailshot they result from. We also have 1,000 leaflets going out in March with the Tumble Tots member pack mailings (which I organised through a company called Independent Direct Marketing). We think this should be well targeted and get a good response. Since Rich has marked all those flyers, we'll know if it works. Our database also allows us to allocate codes to customers to identify which mailing (or whatever) they contacted us from.

3 March

We had a piece in *The Observer* yesterday. It was about a half page – not a review but a kind of columnists piece about the book and then about this particular columnist trying out the methods in the book on her four boys. It was a nice piece; inevitably more about her than about the book, but we'd been expecting that. Irritatingly there wasn't really anything we could pull out as a quote. Elie phoned in the evening to say she'd seen the article – which was really nice of her and helped us feel more excited about it. She says they deliberately avoid writing anything you can quote.

Our first proper phone order! A chap from Ireland who had read *The Observer* piece yesterday rang and ordered a copy. Very exciting. I discovered that I couldn't begin to find my way around the order forms we'd designed, which flustered me slightly. I just took down whatever information I thought I needed and entered it on the form later. A useful discovery – we'll redesign them if necessary before anyone else but us has to use them.

Rich called me to say one of the parents on the school run said they'd seen our piece in *Devon Today*. Interesting, as I didn't know the issue was out yet. He picked up a copy and it's a nice double page spread with a photo (yuk) and a big cover shot of the book. It also gives our details for ordering.

Still no phones. BT seem incapable of telling me what is actually going on. It seems (I don't know if this is right) that each morning they put the job out for either the exchange engineers or the field engineers. If whoever gets it takes a look and decides it's the other department's job, it can't go out to them until the next morning. Then they announce that it was the first department's job after all, and back it goes again for the next day.

The frustrating thing is that I get the impression that most of the engineers are perfectly capable of fixing either field or exchange faults, but they aren't allowed to – they have to stick to their own job. This means that no one takes responsibility for the repair, as they can keep dumping it on each other – and losing 24 hours in the process every time.

Anyway, we have only one White Ladder line, and we can't transfer calls. Only one of us can answer the phone at once – a second caller just gets call minder. So we've plugged in a cordless phone to Rich's working line this morning, while he's out, and I have the receiver bit up in my office. Only I don't get reception there, so I put the phone in my bedroom (which is the next room) so it rings. Then when I answer it, I have to go into the bathroom to get a clear enough reception to talk.

4 March (a.m.)

Elie and Rachael have come up trumps with a foreign rights agent. She currently works part time as foreign rights manager for a publisher, but wants to go freelance after her second child is born in the summer. Bizarrely, you can only really sell foreign rights twice a year: at the London Book Fair in March or – better – at the Frankfurt Book Fair in October. We're a bit late now for the London Book Fair, so she can get going in October at Frankfurt. Rights sales are such a slow process that, although it's a drag waiting six months, it probably won't make a lot of difference in the long run.

We do have an alternative. Another publisher friend recommended a rights agent who is also, by all accounts, excellent. She owns a big rights agency. We'll talk to both of them but our feeling is that we'd rather be with someone smaller. It makes us a more important customer.

GOLDEN RULE: *Where all else is equal, aim to use smaller suppliers.* There may be other factors here but, if you have a choice of good suppliers, you'll get more empathy from fellow small businesses, and you'll be more important to them.

I had a phone call this morning from a columnist on The Times. I've never spoken to him before but we know of each other because we both write for the same publishers. Anyway, he saw the piece in The Observer and wants to include something about *Kids & Co* in his column on Thursday week.

THE NATIONAL PRESS

It had never dawned on me that getting a piece in the paper would attract other journalists – I had only the readers in mind. Dealing with the national press has been a real eye-opener. Here are the main things I've learned:

- It's generally better to email press releases than to post them.
- Phoning before you send the press release means people are more likely to notice it.
- It's worth phoning people after sending the press release – it jogs their memories, and often they haven't seen the email for some reason so you can resend it.
- If you email them you'll never get a reply unless they're very keen.
- ...but they hardly ever answer their phones. Either persist or give up, depending on how important they are to you.
- Most journalists take days to read an email, let alone respond to it. I've taken to giving them about five days before

I make a follow-up call, and even then I sometimes find they haven't read the thing yet. However, if they've asked for information they'll generally read it sooner, so I guess they go through their inboxes daily but only pick out what they want to and save the rest for later.

- The national papers are all made up of dozens of autonomous departments which have no idea what each other is doing. It's no good thinking that you've got a particular paper covered because you emailed, say, the features editor. Your press release will never have gone anywhere near the review section, the Saturday magazine, the business section and so on. There's a certain competitiveness between departments so while some will pass things on to certain other departments, most will keep a press release to themselves, even if they don't want to use it.

- The editors fully expect you to contact other sections of their own newspaper, so you can freely email as many sections as you feel are worth it. The others will probably never know, care or even notice if you get the coverage.

- No one wants old news. If a product launches on a particular date, they won't be interested in covering the story beyond the week of the launch.

- Some papers want an exclusive. This means they will only run a piece if you agree not to allow any other paper to run a similar article until after theirs. This generally applies to big features, and they are generally concerned only with other national papers, and only with feature articles. In our case, *The Times Magazine* don't mind reviews and articles, but don't want another big feature. The potential pitfalls are twofold: firstly, the date of features can move around so having agreed, in our case, not to allow any competing articles before 8 March, they then changed the date to 15 March. We were lucky – what if we'd already agreed a feature for someone else on the 9th? Secondly, you're almost always going to be taking a gamble. Suppose, in our case, the Mail on Sunday had wanted to do a big feature – we'd have regretted giving *The Times Magazine* an exclusive. On the other hand, the *Mail on Sunday* might not want a feature (indeed, they didn't), so we'd regret turning down *The Times Magazine* for a better deal which didn't materialise. All I can say here is that you can't avoid gambling. Weigh up the chances of a better feature coming off, and hope you make the right decision. We felt the most important thing was to avoid ending up with nothing, so we said yes to *The Times Magazine* – which is after all a damn good article to get.

We've abandoned the idea of labels for our envelopes: Rich has realised that we can use the rubber stamps we had made with our logo and address and phone details on. They work fine on the back of the envelope, and much easier and cheaper.

I started using a small company a couple of years ago who make stick on and iron on name labels. I can't be doing with sewing on school name tapes, so I use these instead. Their stick on labels are great for shoes and lunchboxes and so on. We've had two people at school ask us in the last week where we get them from, so we thought we'd call up and ask for a bundle of leaflet/order forms for the school to give out.

Then it occurred to Rich that, since these people obviously mail out to parents all the time, we should ask them to mail out our flyers for us. Only we can't afford to pay for inserts at the moment. So I suggested we see if they'd do a swap – we'll mail out their leaflets in our

books in exchange for them mailing out our flyers. Let's hope they
go for it.

Rich phoned me five minutes ago to say that he's just taken an order
from someone in response to the *She* magazine offer (they told me
this issue wasn't out for another two days). So we're expecting a
handful of orders from that over the next few days. Don't know how
many... I'll guess 30 and we'll see if I'm anywhere close.

4 March (p.m.)

We've just lost another phone line. The other business featureline
number. We can call out but incoming calls all seem to be routed
straight to BT Call Minder without ever ringing at our end. This
means that my personal number is the only one left, apart from
Rich's fax/modem line which has no extensions anywhere but in his
study.

I rang BT and asked them to divert calls to my personal number –
there being nothing else. This means, however, that if we're using
that one line, any caller will simply get an engaged signal. So I asked
BT to put Call Minder on that number just until they get the fault
fixed – which they are now saying will be by next Monday (that's six
days away). I was told it would take two to three days to set up, and
I'd have to pay. I could always try to negotiate a rebate with the sales
department later (some hope). I didn't see why I should have to pay
under the circumstances, rebate or no rebate.

Eventually I ran out of time arguing the toss with them, and had to
go and pick the boys up from school. I asked Rich to call them and

read the riot act. If necessary, even tell them I'm a journalist and keeping notes (true – but it's a good line anyway). By the time I got home, Rich had miraculously got Call Minder up and running, free of charge, on my number. I don't know how he did it, but he spoke to a supervisor (BT like to call them 'leaders') and explained how very upset we are. You'd think that under the circumstances BT would bend over backwards to help, but unfortunately you have to fight even for a small 'goodwill gesture' like this. Anyway, we found out that you don't necessarily *have* to wait two to three days for Call Minder; they can get it set up in five minutes if they want to. Interesting.

I tried to buy a copy of *She* but it turns out it's not in the shops yet – the woman who ordered from us must be a subscriber and have an advance copy.

Radio Dublin read the *Observer* piece and might want an interview – one customer so far and three journalists from that article. Also, I emailed *You and Yours* (BBC Radio 4) who emailed straight back and are really interested but can't find a slot. They're keeping the details on file, they say, until a suitable discussion or item comes up. *Woman's Hour* are coming back to me within a day or two – they put *Kids & Co* forward for a piece next week, but the producer wasn't sure if it got the final go-ahead or not. She'll let me know. All very exciting, and a bit overwhelming. Especially when you've barely got any phones.

5 March

We decided that we would sell books direct – phone, post or website – without charging postage. That way it costs people no more than buying from a bookshop. We do charge an extra £1 for overseas postage. It turns out that overseas postage is fairly expensive, which we should have checked out in advance, but didn't. The book our mate Charlie in Australia ordered cost us £2.40 to post. And the order I took on Monday from Ireland cost us £1.89 (although Rich clean forgot to put the extra postage on it – but we asked at the village post office who said it would turn up anyway, and they were sure the customer wouldn't be asked to pay the excess, because Rich had 'showed willing' by putting 72p on it).

Anyway, we're considering increasing our standard overseas postage to £1.50 – it's easier, especially on the website, if it's always the same. Meantime, Rich has calculated exactly what it actually costs us to post out a single book. We use white envelopes which aren't the cheapest but look by far the smartest. They're by no means the most expensive either – sort of mid range. We also send out a flyer (so people can order another copy or pass the flyer on), and a leaflet inviting them to distribute flyers for us. So here's the total cost:

Bubble bag	0.64
Stamp @ first class	0.72
Book (3090 @ 2248.62)	0.73
Leaflet (1000 @ 70.00)	0.07
Flyer (10,000 @ 338.90)	0.03
Total	2.19
Price	6.99
Gross profit	**£4.80**

It would be a little cheaper, of course, if we were to buy bubble bag envelopes in bulk. At the moment, however, we have neither the cash flow nor the storage space for this. Actually, I suppose we could store them under beds and in wardrobes and generally hidden around the house (away from small children) but not until we can afford to buy them.

BT are going to fix the phones next Monday. Apparently they have to replace a telegraph pole which entails getting people from several different departments together, which can't be organised in under seven days. Of course, there's no guarantee that changing the pole next Monday will actually fix the problem.

Rich spoke to Graham Howe, our accountant, today. He can't face doing the accounts (Rich, that is, not the accountant) so he's paying for a bookkeeper to do them for us. It's going to cost us £52-odd each time for someone to come out for a couple of hours once a fortnight. Rich mentioned the phones to Graham, and said, "BT really ought to make a bit more effort, particularly considering Roni's keeping a journal of everything involved in starting the business, which we'll publish next year" (that's this book here, folks). Graham replied, "Oh my God. Are we in it? I'd better call you every couple of days to check everything's OK."

Unfortunately, *Woman's Hour* couldn't fit us into their schedule next week. Shame. Once publication date has passed they won't touch it, of course. Still, a very nice answerphone message from the producer.

Rich has spoken to the woman who sells name tapes, and she's very happy to send out each other's flyer/order forms. They also help schools to fundraise by giving them 20% of any income generated by the school distributing their leaflets. So they're a company after our own hearts. Let's hope we're both useful for each other.

The woman who Rich took an order from yesterday – the one who had seen the offer in *She* – phoned up today about being a leaflet distributor (we must think of a good name for them). She seemed very keen, so we're putting some flyers in the post to her.

6 March (a.m.)

Interview for the local paper this morning, and a photographer. I hate having my photo taken. They seem to be more than happy to photograph my double chin as though it was an intrinsic part of me. Whereas, of course, it's actually an alien entitiy which mysteriously took up residence at the bottom of my face a few years ago and doesn't deserve any publicity at all.

The phones are getting us down. We started last week on a real high, buzzing and excited. But BT have ground us down to the point where we're both finding that worry and stress have overtaken the excitement. It's their lack of action, their appearing not to care, and their total lack of urgency. Not to mention almost never getting to talk to the same person twice. It's such a shame because starting a business is one of those things you probably only do once in your life, and we should be having a riot – we were until the phone lines started dropping out, one by one, like some telecoms disaster movie. Now the fun has been spoilt, and we'll never be in this situation again. It feels a bit like having someone ruin your wedding.

I'm having problems with Call Minder, too. I'm haunted by the thought that someone could be trying to get through *while I'm dialling up 1571*. Rich says not to go there.

...ed mailing big companies to see if they'll buy *Kids & Co* to ...r employees when they go on maternity or paternity leave. ...ng to the head of human resources in each case, on the basis that it's best to go to the top and they can always pass it down the line for dealing with. Then it kind of carries their approval and the person whose desk it lands on is more likely to do something about it if it comes from top management.

I'm approaching companies who I know have a reputation for being good to their staff, especially when it comes to balancing work and family life. So I have the *Sunday Times 100 best companies to work for* supplement (which happened to come out two weeks ago), and also companies listed on websites such as parentsatwork.org.uk (who give awards for best employers) and employersforwork-lifebalance.org.uk (who give case studies of all their members).

I'm sending a copy of the book to each one, because it only costs us £1 plus the postage and I figure it's worth it – some of these companies could in theory buy hundreds of copies. And I reckon they'll feel that in exchange for a free book, they should at least reply to the accompanying letter.

I'm starting with about half a dozen or so companies. If it gets no response, I might stop sending out the books. My biggest problem at the moment is that I can't go online to research the companies without cutting off our only incoming line in order to plug my modem into it. This phone problem interferes with everything.

The BT contractors have arrived – four days early – to change the telegraph pole. Interestingly, there are just two people, both from the same company. We were told we had to wait several days because the exercise would entail bringing together lots of people from different departments. We were also told it could take days to get permission from the landowner, although I had told BT that the landowner is a very co-operative next-door neighbour who is happy for them to help themselves to access any time. So all in all, I can't see why they couldn't have done this on Monday. But they didn't, anyway.

The contractors are changing the telegraph pole because they've been asked to. This entails disconnecting all our remaining phones for a couple of hours. One of them does say, however, that if this turns out to fix the problem: "I'll eat my hat."

Rich has emailed me an update of what he's been doing for the last week or so (in one of those rare windows when we have internet access). Here it is:

PROGRESS REPORT

The bank's swipe machine is installed and now I am getting the hang of it, it is very easy to use. When a customer phones and you take all their details it takes but a second to tap them into the machine which then goes 'on line' to the bank and confirms acceptance of the card details. At the end of the day you have to swipe your supervisor card and you get a daily total. During the night the machine is 'emptied' by the bank phoning up and doing so automatically. The money gets entered on the bank statement the same day.

WorldPay I still can't get them to email me with the customer's details – all I get is an email saying a sale has been made and what the amount is. I then have to log on to see who ordered what and where they are. Still we're getting there slowly.

Statistics I have been able to access the admin site that deals with 'hits' – who has visited the website, when and what they looked at. In time I think this will be very valuable indeed. At the moment we aren't getting enough hits to extrapolate much info but give it time. It tells me where they came from – i.e. what website they were using when they came across us – how long they looked at each page for, what pages they didn't look at. It's brilliant and I think, as I say, a very valuable tool in time to come.

Cost of printing business stationery It is very expensive to have invoices printed in triplicate with company logo, colours and addresses on. I tried buying a pre-printed pad but it looked crap. Cheapest option so far is to design and print them on computer as and when we need them. They look smart and do what I need them to do which is provide an invoice, a delivery note and a back up copy for me. I could get them from Sage but it's expensive.

Sage is proving a bit of a problem. I can access all the information I've put in but I can't put any more in. I'm sure it is one of those tiny things that when shown I'll go 'Oh, of course, you just hit the enter button or something'. I have elected to employ a bookkeeper. She is delivered from and by accountancy firm. She costs £13 an hour which seems very reasonable to me. She will come in for half a day a fortnight. This gives us 4 hours. I reckon it will take her 2 hours-ish to enter stuff, which will the give her two more hours to answer all my questions.

VAT I have done the Vat and we are owed £900 by the Vat office. I really like this system and hope they never put Vat on books – sorry, they already have it, it just happens to be rated at 0%. Silly me, completely different from books being Vat exempt.

Websites I have been emailing all parenting websites that sell books to try to get a review or sell through the site. Results have been very poor. A few have taken up offer of a review copy and one has posted a good review. One said it will but I do check every few days and no review so far. Of the others I ain't heard back despite emailing them to ask how they got on with the book. Many websites don't even bother replying. I have emailed them at least five times with lots of info – press releases, details of our up and coming media coverage, that sort of thing. They don't respond, not even to tell me to stop sending stuff. Strange. I have got a friend to email them and ask them if they are going to stock *Kids & Co* and quite a few have emailed back to say they have never heard of it. Stranger and stranger. One emailed back to say it was on Amazon at £6.99 which means we must have done a deal with them but the 'street price' would be £8.99 or £9.99, and they would be charging £9.99. Odd when the bloody price is printed on it quite clearly at £6.99.

Baby and child catalogues All the ones who have shown an interest say they are reviewing their catalogues in March and we are up for inclusion. This is JoJoMamanBebe, GLTC and Urchin. Blooming Marvellous said a straight no – they don't carry books – which at least is decisive and up front.

WH Smith, Mothercare and Adams Another strange tale. I phone them up and ask 'Who should I send a book to?' I explain we are a new company etc. I get given a name. I send the book off for review/inclusion in their stores. After a day or two I chase – phone up, email etc. I can never get through. After seven attempts – leaving messages etc – I phone reception again and ask the same question: 'Who should we send the book to if we want the stores to stock it?'. I always get given a different name. I begin again. I send the book. I chase. I leave messages. I would have thought new products were their bread and butter, but apparently they are all so unavailable they can't be stocking anything. If they don't want the book I do wish they would follow the excellent example of Blooming Marvellous and just say so outright and save me a whole lot of stress.

I did phone BabyGap and ask who I should talk to. I was given a strange phone number that began with a lot of 00000's. I phoned and asked and was told they didn't stock books, ever. And then I realised I was talking to someone in America. Hope I got them out of bed.

So, everything is in place. We are all geared up and ready to go. All our systems are tested and OK. All we need now are the phones to work properly and we could be selling books. I don't think BT realise how harmful this is to our nerves, mental health, business and general optimism. Compensation? I should think so but I would rather not have the stress. I could do without it, thank you very much.

7 March (a.m.)

Well, it's good news for yesterday's telephone contractor: he won't have to eat his hat. Changing the pole has made not the slightest difference. I was told last night by BT that someone would turn up on Monday, but after making a lot of fuss I persuaded them to send someone today instead. Actually, every time either of us speaks to BT today we're told, "They'll be along to change the pole on Monday." When we patiently explain that the pole has been changed already, they are totally stumped and don't know what to say.

We did get an engineer this morning, at about 11.45. He has no idea of any of the history, and thought only one number was faulty. Our work is already seriously curtailed by the phone problem, and I can't go online at all for all the research I want to do into corporates without disconnecting the only incoming line to plug my modem into it. So the work has to be shelved. Every engineer that comes out then eats up even more of our frantically pressured time having to be shown round, given a guided tour of all the poles in the field at the back of the house etc etc.

Now the two remaining lines have both gone very crackly – alarmingly that's exactly what the others did before they went completely dead. Rich got so irritated with BT that he phoned up again. He was kept waiting for 10 minutes to speak to someone. Then he got one of the ones that sighs at you. They make it so clear that they aren't in the least interested in your problems, and wish you'd keep them to yourself. She actually said to Rich, "Your phone obviously works, because you're talking to me."

The Times have delayed our feature again – don't know when to.

TIME ELAPSED 9 months 1 weeks 0 days

I've been emailing magazines which go to teachers and PTAs with a press release about *Kids & Co*, mentioning the fact that schools can fundraise by getting £2 back from us for every copy ordered through them. I hope we get some coverage of this, and some response.

7 March (p.m.)

Right. BT have said they're now putting this on top priority. Give me strength. They sent another engineer round this afternoon, and I wasted another 45 minutes showing him all the bits of phones he wanted to see. He'd been given the wrong information about what lines were and weren't working. Anyway, he seemed to know what he was doing by the end of it, and thinks he's worked out where the fault must be. I'm not holding my breath.

A couple of days ago I emailed Nicola Horlick, who is CEO of SG Asset Management, to ask if she would consider endorsing *Kids & Co* if I sent her a copy. It would be a great endorsement for encouraging big companies to buy the book. I got a lovely email back from her today saying she'd be delighted to take a look at the book, and please send her a copy. It's in the post – I just hope she likes it.

GOLDEN RULE: *Don't be afraid to ask for endorsements.* The right person can add immense credibility to your product and people don't mind being asked. The worst they can do is politely decline, and you'd be surprised how many will say yes.

10 March

We have phones! At last. We were out all day on Saturday, and when we got back the phones were fixed. We both feel immensely happier and more relaxed as a result.

We had a great article in the *Western Morning News* on Saturday, with a photo of us and the kids, a shot of the book, and an offer to order by phone and get £1 off.

The only thing is, we're getting very few orders here, by phone or by post. We're getting pretty nervous, to be honest. Is this normal, or is it a sign of trouble? We'll just have to wait and see if it picks up.

I did an interview for a reviewer at the *Daily Record* this morning. She loves the book and I think will give us a great review. The *Daily Record* sells in huge numbers in Scotland – it's one of the biggest selling papers with a readership of well over half a million.

11 March

We're now debating compensation with BT. Or, rather, trying to debate it but they won't negotiate. They used to, but now they pay at a fixed rate. What's more, that rate reduces drastically if the faulty line is diverted, since they say this means you weren't without a service. In our case we had three lots of calls coming in on a single number meaning the line was frequently blocked, and we didn't have facilities like transferring calls.

I was also obliged to take calls in the bathroom at times – out of reach of all my paperwork, computer etc – and I had no internet or email access without blocking the only business line. Nevertheless, as far as BT is concerned, we had service so compensation is at a minimum. They have offered us, for each of the two business numbers, £9.33 a day for the eight days they were out of order. That's a total of £149.33 for the entire experience.

Meanwhile, GLTC, one of the parents mail order catalogues, has decided not to take *Kids & Co*.

The article in the Western Daily Press has so far generated one order and two manuscripts from local poets wanting us to publish their verses. I've politely said no, obviously.

Our biggest frustration at the moment is Amazon. Funny how we've found all the small businesses we've dealt with to be a dream, while all the big organisations are a nightmare. Anyway, Rich keeps joining the Amazon Advantage scheme for small publishers – which you have to join online – only to find that it hasn't taken effect and *Kids & Co* is listed as 'usually despatched in 4-6 weeks'. I think he has finally got it sorted – he sent me this email update.

After six weeks of trying our book has finally been released by amazon.co.uk (rather than listed as 'not yet published') but disastrously is listed as being available in 4 to 6 weeks. I tried phoning to no avail. The woman just kept trying to give me the email address of their Advantage scheme (to whose advantage?). When I said I was in the scheme but that they didn't reply to emails she again tried to give me the email address. She said I wasn't allowed to talk to them.

I did email and complain about the 4 to 6 weeks and the

emailed reply said to join the advantage scheme! Argh! Anyway, I have eventually managed to join the scheme – it seems that each application was rejected because I entered our distributor's details. You have to have a distributor to join, but Amazon don't want to know about them – they want to order direct from us. Sorted now, but it will take 1-2 weeks for *Kids & Co* to show up on the system as being despatched promptly.

Insurance

Alton Logistic have sent a bill for £122 for insurance for our books in storage at their warehouse. I thought it was going to be around £54 as the quote was for £18 per thousand pounds value and we have three thousand books worth about £1 each. Oh no. The stock isn't valued at cost – roughly a pound a book – but at 2/3rds of retail price (which comes to £249, so why we are only being charged at a rate of about $^1/_3$ of retail I have no idea).

When I pointed out to Allan that I had expected the insurance to be valued at cost he said no. I said, "So that means we get a decent pay off if your place burns down? In fact we get a better deal than if we sold all our books to Gardners? And we get it in bulk." I told Allan to watch his place at night. He said he'd never thought of that.

We can't work out why we're getting so few orders, unless people just don't like buying books by phone or direct from the publisher generally. In this case they'll go to bookshops – and Gardners have ordered 100 copies so that should work fine – or else they'll try to order from Amazon. That's why we really want to get Amazon sorted promptly. Anyway... so much for fretting about how we'd handle all the calls. I feel slightly embarrassed now for even worrying about it.

> **GOLDEN RULE:** *When you have to deal with bureaucracy, you can't beat persistence.* It's a matter of being dogged, finding the right person or system, and just sticking at it. It's worth it in the end.

12 March

Spoke to Mark Allin this morning about tomorrow's editorial board meeting for the first three titles next year – he may not be able to make it to the meeting so he was feeding in his key comments just in case. He also told us not to worry about the level of orders – that's fine for where we're at right now, he says, and should pick up. That's a relief.

I've had an email from *The Times* to say that the article will be in on 22 March. I do hope it doesn't get moved again.

After lunch, all our phone lines went down except for Rich's private line. I burst into tears. I sobbed at some poor BT engineer for ages down the phone while he tested all the lines. In the end they said they could fix my fax/modem line on Friday, the Featureline numbers on Saturday (it's Wednesday today) and my domestic line and Rich's fax/modem next Thursday. This is patently daft since they all have the same fault. However the poor operator – who was very sympathetic – did mark all the jobs priority when he heard the problems we'd had lately.

He also told me that you can subscribe to something called TotalCare for £9.99 a quarter which means that you get to queue jump everyone else and BT work round the clock on any repairs. No one had ever mentioned this to us before. "Great!" I said. "I'll have it!" Oh, no. Apparently you can't sign up for it when there's a fault on the line. At the current rate we'll be lucky to find a window at all when we can register.

Anyway, by pure chance we happened to have an engineer here at the time. Rich had asked for someone to cut back some tree branches which were threatening to cause problems with the line sooner or later. I headed out into the garden when I first discovered that all our lines were dead and asked if he could do anything about it. I said, "It's a higher priority than cutting back the tree." He said, "I'm afraid it doesn't work like that."

However, he very kindly said when he left that he'd drive back along the route of the line and look out for any trouble. Twenty minutes later he phoned and said he'd checked out an old troublespot and found the wires were dodgy. He'd reconnected them and could we check the phones? We did, and they were all working. What a star! I'd better sign up to TotalCare quick before I miss my chance.

14 March

We went to London yesterday for our editorial board meeting, which was incredibly useful. Unfortunately Mark didn't make it, but I had all his comments to feed in to the meeting anyway. We had three books up for discussion, all for publication at the beginning of next year:

- *Climbing the Ladder* That's this book you've got in your hand now. The general view was that it was a great idea but the title needed tweaking – it sounded a bit like a career book. So we need to find something that indicates starting a business more clearly, or at least is less associated with careers, and then give it a subtitle which tells clearly what the book is about. Also we need to make it clear in the presentation of the book that it's about starting up specifically – not about maintaining a successful business. We also discussed price – so if you feel you've paid too much for this book, blame our editorial board, not us.

- *Babies for Beginners* This is a humorous but very accurate and practical guide to the absolute essentials of coping with babies. It should appeal to all new parents, including fathers who traditionally read far less about babycare than mothers do. This won a resounding thumbs-up from the board, who also had some useful comments about possible marketing channels.

- *Licking Death* This was the most controversial title. It's a personal journal by Rich – similar in style to *The Voice of Tobacco* – about learning to be less afraid of death. It will be full of strategies and techniques that other people use to face death with more equanimity, including people who work in the field – religious leaders, health professionals and so on. We had proposed a cover with an image of a skull on (no pussy-footing around for us) but the board persuaded us that there are two markets for the book: people who are facing relatively imminent death (theirs or someone close) and people who want to overcome a general fear of death, of the kind that strikes around the age of 40 to 45. If we want to appeal to those who are facing death in the near future, we need to avoid anything stark and scary. So we have to change our cover design for this one, and the title – we are thinking of calling it *The Joy of Death* since we hope it will help to break down the taboo of death in the way that *The Joy of Sex* broke down the taboo of sex in the 60s.

We also discussed the pack we send out to customers. As well as the book they get their credit card receipt, an order form, a leaflet inviting them to recommend the book and earn £2 for every order they generate, and an Easy2name leaflet. Is this too much? Or could we send out more? The verdict was that we could probably include up to 5 things – and that it was odd to send out an order form for the book they've just bought so we should drop that. That means we can accommodate up to two more things. One will be the bookmark (ready next week), so we could find one more small but relevant business to do a reciprocal mailing with.

After the meeting we met our potential foreign rights agent. She's pregnant at the moment and will decide in the summer probably, once she's on maternity leave from her present job, whether she wants to go freelance or not. We're hoping she will, because we think she would be perfect. We liked her enormously, she's bright and on the ball, really knows her stuff, and comes highly recommended by Rachael and Elie. We agreed that we'll use the replacement agent for the next few months and see how we get on – if it doesn't work out and she does go freelance we can always switch over later.

We paid someone to spend all day at home for us answering the phone if it rang – we didn't like to leave the White Ladder phone all day. When we got back we discovered that we had wasted our money completely – BT had failed to take off the divert on the White Ladder phone as we'd asked them to the night before. So all White Ladder calls went through to Rich's residential number (which we had asked Anne not to answer) and got his personal answerphone message which obviously doesn't mention White Ladder at all. There were a couple of confused messages from people saying they were unsure if they'd got the right number. BT had diverted four lines on Wednesday and had successfully removed the divert on the other three, but not on the one that actually mattered. I'm now claiming for the money we wasted paying Anne.

More encouraging was coming home to two orders in the post, one of them an order form sent out for us by Easy2name, the nametape people who are doing a reciprocal mailing with us.

> By the way, if you have children and hate sewing on name tapes, I can thoroughly recommend Easy2name. You can call them on 01635 298326.

Rich has been putting together a page of quotes from our reviews. We'll send this out to independent bookshops (faxing them apparently works best) to let them see that *Kids & Co* should generate interest. Matthew advises that we can offer to sell them copies direct at a better discount than they get from the wholesalers, but on firm sale only, not sale or return – and with a sliding discount rate.

I've done two phone interviews for local radio stations today, and we had a good review in the local paper – a whole page and very complimentary about the book.

I talked to a magazine editor today about doing a special offer on *Kids & Co* when she reviews it in her magazine. I suggested our usual offer – £1 off – and she said she didn't think that sounded good enough to be worth doing. Interesting. I wonder if the low response to offers in *She* and *Western Morning News* and so on might be due to the offer not being enticing enough. I think we'll review this and maybe give £2 off (for instance) in future, especially if some of our titles will have a higher cover price. Anyway, this particular magazine was sorted out because we agreed that we'd give away the first five copies free, and then give everyone else £1 off.

18 March

I've decided to fax independent schools – similarly to Rich faxing bookshops. I'll send them a brief selection of reviews, a synopsis, and invite them to use the book to fundraise. For every book we sell through them, we give them back £2. I'm currently getting hold of listings of independent schools. Actually, maybe I should mail instead of fax. I could put in a bit more information, and a copy of the flyer. Hmmm.

Matthew and Sarah faxed us through a photocopy of the ad Gardners put in their latest catalogue that they send to bookshops. They did a third of a page about *Kids & Co*, with a cover shot and so on, so let's hope they get a fair few orders.

I've been phoning round the corporates I sent copies of *Kids & Co* to, proposing they buy copies to give to staff on maternity and paternity leave. So far one has asked for a telephone meeting next Monday, one has said no (it's too complicated to organise because they have so many staff), and the others have all passed the book on to other people – junior to them – to deal with. This is quite promising. Oh, and one is considering it as part of a maternity package redesign they're doing, and won't have an answer for a couple of months – which means they're considering it. Also, Video Arts (who make the John Cleese training films) may be interested in distributing it when they expand the book side of their operations later in the year.

We're slightly nervous that orders are still a bit thin on the ground. They're running at one or two a day now, which I suppose is heading the right way, but very slowly. We did get a call though from someone who had bought a copy, asking for 250 leaflets to distribute to a group she runs, to raise money for the local hospice.

21 March

On second thoughts, I'll mail schools rather than fax them. That means I can include more than one sheet of paper (though I don't want to deluge them). I'd like to add a copy of the flyer so they can see what it looks like.

It's difficult finding time for all this, and I'm starting to be very picky about what I spend time on. I need to be more ruthless. I'm back to work next month – the day job, writing a book for another publisher – because I can't afford to take any more time off from earning. My general approach with schools, corporates etc is to approach a decent-sized sample, say 30 or 40, and see what happens. This doesn't take too long, but it's enough to get an idea of success or otherwise. Then if it looks promising I'll keep going; if it doesn't I drop it and put my time into something else.

I've done almost nothing for two days, because Rich has been laid up with a horrendous migraine – even the morphine the doctor finally gave him had no effect – so I've been looking after the children on his shifts as well as mine. Exhausting, but actually I've rather enjoyed having extra time with Hal in the mornings. However, it does nothing for the workload; I've kept on top of post and emails etc, but that's about all.

It makes me realise how vulnerable White Ladder is with only two of us. What if we both come down with the same bug? Or have a serious family crisis? We'll both work through pretty much anything – we almost never take time off – but when it does happen it leaves us with no cover at all for the business.

I have found time to email the editorial board with a choice of three titles for this book: *Launching the Ladder*, *New Tricks for Old Dogs*, and *The White Ladder Diaries* (which seems to be favourite from the responses so far). We've also decided (Rich and I) that we prefer the orignial idea for *Licking Death* – it's more White Ladderish – and we don't want to water it down even though this will broaden the market. So we're going to save it for a year or two until we have more titles and can better afford to take a risk on a new title without the business's success depending on it. Right now we're worried enough about the sparse orders without publishing a book that may not work.

We've also been looking for a name to give all our sales people who are customers we've sent flyers to who then earn commission on sales they generate. We were reluctant to use partners – our best idea to date – because it's a bit formal and businesslike. We wanted something more quirky and with a touch of humour. So we came up with Barkers – obviously it relates to the old dogs thing, and also the idea of a fairground barker who calls out to round people up for the show. We'd put a dictionary definition of 'barker' at the bottom of the cover of our 'welcome pack' so the reasoning would be clear. So far, our two editorial board members who've got back to us on this both like the idea.

24 March

What an exciting day! Our feature was in *The Times* magazine on Saturday (and a nice piece in the Plymouth *Evening Herald* too). We were very pleased with it – the photo of me was quite ghastly, but the children looked so adorable (which is probably why they picked that picture) that I doubt anyone would notice what I looked like. They ran an offer, too, through their own system which we couldn't work out how they were organising since we hadn't heard anything from them.

Anyway, today is Monday. And the phone was very busy this morning. For a start, the people who organise *The Times* reader offers called. Apparently they wait until they get a response before they worry about getting hold of the book. Over the weekend, they had 40 orders (which they say is very good) and they hoped this would turn into about 80-100 by the end of today (lots of people wait until Monday to call). They had called our distributor, who was apparently quite unhelpful and refused to give them credit since they didn't have an account with them. So they called us instead, and talked to Rich (who is seeing the distributor tomorrow morning to find out what happened and sort out what happens in future).

It turns out that these people who run the offer for *The Times* are in fact none other than The Book People. This organisation more significantly operates like a book club, only it's not a club as such, and sells discounted books through the post, on the Internet and through reps who call at offices. Rich has been trying since January to get them to buy *Kids & Co* and has made very little headway. They have a copy, they don't get back to him, he chases and can't get the person he wants – usual story. But the person he spoke to about The Times offer thought The Book People really should sell *Kids & Co* and seemed keen to persuade her colleagues to take the book on. So let's hope it has some effect.

I'm starting to get the hang of the system now. Media coverage is what really generates more media coverage. As a result of the piece in *The Times*, *This Morning* rang and asked for a review copy. They had, in fact, turned down the idea about two weeks ago (after taking it as far as shortlisting it for the week of publication). But a completely different person called up today. And then *Richard & Judy* called and asked if I would be free for this Thursday's show. It's not definite yet, but looking likely. Like features in the nationals, whichever daytime TV show you say yes to asks you not to do any others until after theirs. So if *Richard & Judy* happens, I couldn't do *This Morning* until later even if they were interested – in which case they'd probably decide they didn't want me after all thanks. I think the only way to play these things is to take whatever comes first – a bird in the hand and all that.

I spoke to an HR-related director of one of the big corporates on the phone this morning (they employ over 100,000 people). She may well be interested in buying in *Kids & Co* as a corporate gift for employees who have a baby. I'm sending her a copy – plus copies of several reviews – and she'll get back to me in a couple of weeks.

Rich has had nil response to his faxes to bookshops last week. He hates chasing up this kind of contact, still being very uncomfortable with aspects of his sales role (though getting extremely adept at other aspects of it). Anyway, I offered to call round half a dozen of the bookshops as a trial, and let him know what sort of response I got. My angle was, "I'm calling to let you know that since we faxed you we've had a feature in *The Times* magazine, and we're going to be on *Richard & Judy* this week." Of the three I got through to, all were positive. Two hadn't seen the fax and asked me to send it again as they were interested. The other had been interested but has just moved to smaller premises and isn't buying in any new stock. But if customers start ordering it she'll buy in copies for stock too. Rich seems happier about calling round a few more himself now over the next few days.

I'm pushed for time at the moment, and I have to write a book for another publisher next month which will mean very little time for White Ladder. But I can't afford not to do any other work, since White Ladder isn't yet bringing in a living wage – or anything approaching it. My two key projects on the *Kids & Co* sales front are approaching corporates (I've only contacted a dozen so far) and mailing schools to encourage them to fundraise by distributing our leaflets and taking a £2 commission on all sales they generate. I can't do both at once, and I may only have time to do one of these two things before I take a month off to write this other book. So which to do?

It has to come down to which of the two is likely to generate more sales for the time I put in. And I reckon that has to be businesses. One contact could potentially generate hundreds of sales, so long as

I'm targeting businesses with thousands of staff. And, crucially, they could keep coming back with more orders as they use up their stock – which isn't going to apply to schools.

> **GOLDEN RULE:** When time is limited, work out the most cost-effective way to spend what time you have.

25 March

We're ranked 508 on amazon.co.uk. At 9am we were ranked 203. It won't last long (it's because of *The Times* piece, obviously) and it actually only indicates a handful of sales, due to the strangeness of Amazon sales fluctuations. But that's not the point! Last week we went from around 78,000 in the rankings to about 53,000, so to leap up the charts like this – however briefly – is very exciting indeed.

Rich saw the distributor this morning – it turns out yesterday's confusion with The Times reader offer was all a misunderstanding. What the distributor actually told them was that they couldn't negotiate discounts with them since only we could do that – quite right too. Anyway, Allan also told Rich that five branches of Waterstones have ordered copies of *Kids & Co.*

The Times reader offer contacted Rich today and ordered 120 copies of *Kids & Co.*

And *Richard & Judy* is going to use the book, but not until next week. They want to find a sample family, film them over the weekend, and then have me go in on Monday and tell the parents – using rules from the book – how they should be dealing with their children. Then they'll have a go at doing it my way. (How can I possibly do that without coming across as ghastly?) Anyway, they'll turn all that into a 2 minute film, and then they'll interview me in the studio for about 5 mins afterwards. The thought makes me cringe and break out in a sweat, but there's no point doing the book if I'm not prepared to promote it when I'm given the chance. At least next time it will be Rich's book, and I can do the PR without having to do the interviews. How I'm looking forward to that.

Rich has been faxing and emailing the edited highlights of our reviews round, and Mothercare have finally got back to us as a result and asked for a copy of the book.

26 March

Six orders in one day! Including one from *She* magazine, one from the *Western Morning News* (a daily paper which we were in 18 days ago), and two from the *Daily Record*, which had a good review in it today and an offer. Also a call from BBC Radio Scotland – who I imagine read the piece in the *Daily Record* – asking me to be on some live morning show next Friday (the morning after *Richard & Judy* the night before).

Our new agent (number four in as many months) came down to meet us today. At last, someone we really feel confident will stick around and sell some foreign rights for us. We've been very straight with him, and told him he has until about October to show us that he can do better than our other option (should she decide to go freelance). We think there's a good chance he'll do very well – he's very switched on, knows what he's doing and has several years' experience of the business.

27 March

Blimey! I had a call from *This Morning*, who want me to do next Wednesday's show. Interesting, because I did say that once I'd agreed to *Richard & Judy*, that was that and I should take whichever came first (since I can't do both). But actually, now it's come to it, I found myself torn. I felt I should stick with what I'd said yes to for ethical reasons, but everyone seems to think that *This Morning* is far better targeted for us. The editor at *This Morning* – who is very persuasive – says it's fine to turn *Richard & Judy* down at this stage; it happens all the time. But then, she would say that. So I took advice.

I asked Elie, who said that *This Morning* was a much better option, and it would be OK to turn down *Richard & Judy*. It's a cut-and-thrust business and they expect these things. Then I asked my father. He used to be editor of the *Tonight* programme back in the 50s – a live daily programme – so I figured he'd know how it felt from their side. He's also very ethical, and if he felt I ought to stick by a commitment to *Richard & Judy* he would say so. In fact he reckoned I should do *This Morning* – it's a hard-nosed business decision really. He said he'd be very apologetic, but point out that we're a new publisher and this is our first book, and we can't afford not to take the best opportunities. If someone had done that to him on *Tonight* he'd have been pissed off, but he wouldn't have held it against them personally. He'd have recognised that it was the best decision for them. He asked if the editor I'd been dealing with at *Richard & Judy* was a man or a woman. I told him she's a woman. "Good," he said. "Less likely to hang up on you."

She didn't hang up on me. I felt dreadful about calling (and the displacement activity before I finally picked up the phone was remarkable – I discovered all sorts of emails that had to be sent urgently, and even emergency filing to do). I can't say she was thrilled, and she tried to persuade me that it was the wrong decision (as anyone in her position would), but she accepted it as graciously as could be expected.

Then I called *This Morning* back, and said yes. The editor was really pleased, and said she'd get back to me in a couple of hours about coming down here to film etc on Monday or Tuesday.

This is all a bit overwhelming to be honest. When we started setting up White Ladder last summer, I really didn't anticipate finding myself in a position where my best option was to turn down the *Richard & Judy* show. I just hope it starts translating into sales, or we're wasting our time.

Total sales so far are about 320. It's getting slightly worrying, and money is getting tight. Both Rich and I get decent royalties from publishers at the end of this month – a few thousand each – but not enough to last us indefinitely. And nothing else much due in for 6 months from elsewhere, so we badly need White Ladder to start pulling in some hard cash as fast as possible. We printed 3,000 copies initially in case we had a rush at the beginning and didn't have time to reprint. But it now looks as though this was completely unnecessary. We're actually extremely confident that we'll sell them eventually. Trouble is, we need to sell them now. Standard terms for publishers royalties is that they are payable every six months (apart from a few bastard publishers who pay once a year). But we are paying royalties 3 monthly. So at the end of May, we pay ourselves royalties on sales from January to the end of March. It's not going to be much.

I don't really like to think about what happens if sales don't pick up. But I feel that we've learnt so much from *Kids & Co* Rich and I would both simply tighten our belts and go ahead with *The Voice of Tobacco* at least before we considered pulling out. After all, a lot of our time has gone into setting up the business, and we could do one more book for relatively little money and without giving up other work. Let's hope it doesn't come to this decision.

Changing the subject, we had a call this morning from a company of sales reps interested in taking us on as a client and selling our books into bookshops – including Waterstones, Ottakars and WH Smith. The guy is coming to see us next week. On the down side, reps take a percentage (along with everyone else). Also, there's a danger they'll over sell and we'll end up with returns, which we really don't want. On the up side, of course, they may get us into places we'd never get otherwise. We'll see how they look when we meet.

31 March

The Times offer people emailed over the weekend to order another 60 copies of the book. And I hope that being on *This Morning* on Wednesday will generate plenty of orders – God knows I wouldn't do it otherwise. So far we have only 6 orders from *She* magazine (I was wrong with that prediction) but they're still trickling in – one came in this morning. The *Western Morning News* has also brought in 6 orders.

TIME ELAPSED 9 months 4 weeks 3 days

Rich has a great line when people phone with orders, and he wants to give the impression we're bigger than we really are. They usually say, "I'd like to order a book," and he replies, "Certainly, which one?" It made me hoot the first time I heard it.

I got my phone bill through from BT today. We're still quibbling over the featureline compensation, but I agreed the compensation they offered for my residential numbers, which was a total of £128. Well, guess what? They billed me by mistake, instead of crediting me. I've spent 25 minutes on the phone this morning (just like old times) to no avail, and they say they'll get back to me when they've sorted it out. They may be some time.

I'm getting very nervous about Wednesday morning. Rich suggested I go and have a beauty treatment tomorrow morning, to relax me and help me feel more confident. I've never had such a thing before and I went through the Yellow Pages with no idea what to look for, but I've booked a session tomorrow morning. I can't really spare the time, but I think it's a great idea so I'm doing it anyway.

I've trawled every book I have which has anything to say about appearing on television. There's a lot of useful stuff, actually. Although *This Morning* is scary because it's live and has about 2 million or so viewers, they're very good to deal with. I know pretty much what questions I'm going to be asked, so I can prepare answers. And for the phone-in, I get to go through the questions that have been phoned in and pick which ones I want to be asked.

I keep reminding myself, too, that the programme and the presenters want to do the piece because they like the idea and the book. They're not in the business of making people look bad; they want me to come across as well as possible, so they'll do all they can to help.

Apart from watching the programme in advance, I've found plenty of hints for coming across well. If you're likely to be challenged on anything controversial you also need to find out about how to handle probing questions. But for feelgood programmes like *This Morning*, here are the best tips I've found:

- Wear something safe and comfortable. Brighten up black with a bit of colour, avoid stripes, checks, and black & white.
- Ask to check the introduction to make sure all the facts are right – name of book, my name etc.
- Take a few deep breaths just before you start – it helps prevent your voice from going squeaky with nerves.
- Remember that the first two seconds will give most people their opinion of you – so smile and look confident. Keep your hands in your lap, don't cross them, or you'll look very defensive.
- Keep both feet on the floor.
- Sit slightly forward, to show interest.
- Focus totally on the interviewer and ignore everything else going on in the studio. Never look at the camera.
- Make eye contact with the interviewer.
- Don't gabble (my biggest problem) or mumble.

You'll be lucky if people remember much, if anything, of what you say. Watch a similar type of interview yourself on TV, and then ask yourself an hour later how much you actually remember. So when it comes to what you'll actually say, here are a few more useful guidelines to make your interview as memorable as possible:

- Prepare the two or three key points you want to make in the introduction.

- Have plenty of anecdotes and concrete examples ready.
- Make sure you know what you most want to say, and say it no matter what they ask you. Find a link – however tenuous – between the question and your answer.
- Come up with one or two key 'sound-bites' you can use which will stick in people's heads. For example (I have to credit my father for this one) "Parenting is an endless exercise in personnel management".
- Don't ramble, or the interviewer will cut you off. Keep all your answers to around 30 seconds, maybe 45, at the most.
- If you want to emphasise a point particularly, say it slower.
- Prepare a summing-up sentence with the thought you want to leave in the viewers' minds.

Well, that's the end of my diary of launching a business. I guess we've arrived now – we're no longer setting up but actually running the company. It may be tentative, and it may be fragile, but this is a live business. We're taking orders, planning our next products, trying to make a name for ourselves.

The last 10 months have been some of the most exciting and the most fun of my life. It may be a while before we know if our fledgling company will take to the skies, but at least we've nursed it this far and I think we've given it the best chance in life that we can. I'm looking forward to the next few years, but I'll miss this stage too – just as you want your children to grow up but you miss the first weeks and months. I think Rich and I have almost the same kind of emotional attachment to White Ladder as we do to our children, albeit not as strong.

The overwhelming feeling I have at this point is that I'm so glad we did it. It would have been easy to say – as I've often done before –

that it's a great idea but maybe I'll do it later, or perhaps someone else should do it. But this time we went right ahead and got on with it. From those first tentative steps, we've gathered momentum and picked up speed, and now we're poised to take off and fly. Watch this space.

Six months on...

TIME ELAPSED months weeks days

Six months on...

22 September

White Ladder Press is so much a part of our lives now that it's hard to remember that a little over a year ago it wasn't even thought of. Today is publication day for our second book, *The Voice of Tobacco*, and a good moment to look back over the last six months and bring you up to date.

They say that it takes around three years to be sure whether you've got a viable business (assuming you last that long, of course) and I think that will probably hold true for us. We're as confident as we can be that we'll get there, but it's slow going and we aren't yet secure. After all, we're only publishing our second title today, and we need to be publishing about 10 a year to be successful.

The bad news

So what did we get wrong? Let's get that out of the way first. Essentially, we were over-optimistic about a number of things:

■ How well the first book would sell
■ How willing people would be to buy books through non-traditional channels
■ What our average discount would be

These were probably our key mistakes. I think our forecasts for sales will turn out to be accurate for future books, but the first few are so much harder to sell. Most people want to buy books from bookshops, even if they can get them cheaper and just as easily elsewhere.

It's been a long slog getting into the shops, and we're still working on it, but things are improving. Gardners, of course, backed us from the start. Now Bertrams, the other big wholesaler, have started stocking our books too. Although this doesn't guarantee that the books go into bookshops, it's a big help. And just last week, WH Smith Travel ordered 250 copies of *The Voice of Tobacco* for their airport and railway station bookshops. Getting into WHS is more than many publishers ever manage so we're delighted. So the trend is in the right direction, and as we build up more of a name so things will improve.

The non-book trade sales have been, frankly, disappointing. We have sold some copies of *Kids & Co* to businesses, and a few through schools, but there is great resistance to buying books unconventionally. It simply isn't cost effective to pursue many of these routes. Likewise, we've had a few responses to order forms which have gone out with other companies' mailings, but the results haven't been inspiring.

We are now looking at selling bulk copies in advance to organisations who will guarantee to take several thousand copies in exchange for either their name on the book, or a substantial discount (or both). This is a tested route, and we've taken on an excellent freelance sales person to do precisely this for us (he used to work with Mark Allin at Capstone). Our last freelance sales person, who approached us specifically to handle non-book trade sales, decided that he wanted only to do trade sales after all. This meant giving him a percentage of what Rich could sell himself, which seemed daft, so we politely separated ourselves from the arrangement.

The fact that people resist buying in non-traditional ways means that our direct sales have been slow. We're selling about ten percent of the books ourselves, and the rest go through the book trade. Reader offers have been less rewarding than we hoped, although *The Times* reader offer (which they run themselves) generated over 300 orders. Other than that, we've had about 60 orders as a result of reader offers. Nothing like as much as we expected.

This low proportion of direct sales has affected our bottom line considerably. We had estimated an average discount of 40 percent, and based all our calculations on that. But in fact, our average discount is over 50 percent (the wholesalers take 55 percent, and Amazon take 60 percent). It makes a big difference.

We're still hopeful that our scheme of getting customers to sell books on and take a commission will work well, but it hasn't really had a chance yet with only one title. Once people can sell ten books or more at once, with fresh titles arriving every few weeks, they have far more chance of doing well out of it. We do have some people selling for us out there, but not enough yet.

The other big problem we've had is that *Kids & Co* is a tricky book to sell. We think we know why (we need to understand what makes our books sell or White Ladder has no chance), and we've avoided the problem with our future titles. The thing is, everyone says it's very 'clever' but no one really feels they *need* it. If you're trying to quit smoking, you'll look at *The Voice of Tobacco* and think "I need that!" Maybe not everyone will, but a lot will. If you're starting a business, I hope you'll look at this book and think, "Just what I need!"

But *Kids & Co* doesn't do that to people. They think, "Interesting. Clever." And they don't buy it. Well, some do of course, and we've even had customers come back for more copies. But not enough. So far we've sold a little over 1,000 copies, although sales are still coming in steadily so that will go up. We think we should have retitled the book, *How To Get Your Children To Do Whatever You Want Without Arguing*. Then parents everywhere would think, "I need that!" (I'm not actually joking; we may yet do that.)

The good news

If this all sounds gloomy, it shouldn't. It's more that our initial optimism has been tempered with realism. But many things have gone extremely well. For a start, Rich turns out to be a whizz at selling, even though he still can't see it. Every time he pulls off a great deal, such as WHS, I say, "See! You can sell!" and he replies, "Yes, but that wasn't really *selling*, was it?"

We have taken on a freelancer, as I said, to handle big sales outside the book trade and so on, and also to find distributors overseas to take the books. This means our own copies, in English, from us. So we don't sell the rights in English speaking countries; we effectively distribute under our own name.

This leaves Rich selling to the wholesalers, big book chains, catalogues and so on. Considering how small we are he's done incredibly well, and he's making progress all the time.

That leads me on to one of our best decisions, which we made quite by accident. You may remember that we printed copies of *Kids & Co* two months early so that Rich had copies in his hand to make the prospect of selling a little less daunting. We reckoned that we could afford it just with the first book. As it turned out, this was a huge advantage, and we've scheduled to do the same thing with every book. It's not only sales – it's the PR too. Journalists and editors don't like to commit to an article until they've seen the book, and almost no non-fiction publishers have advance copies except for very highly promoted titles. However, we can steal a march on the rest of them because we have finished copies ready at least eight weeks before publication.

We've done terrifically well with PR. *Kids & Co* has had reviews or articles in over 35 publications so far, with several still to come. The final total will be around 50 by the end of the year. These have included *The Times, The Observer, The Times Educational Supplement, She, Woman, Junior, Eve* and many more. The reviews have been almost without exception excellent (one moderate, two poor, all the rest full of praise). In addition, I did several local and regional radio interviews, local TV and, of course, *This Morning*. After all the nerves right up until I went on, it was easy when it came to it and I could almost say I enjoyed it. Almost.

The Voice of Tobacco is heading the same way. It is officially published today, as I said, but has already had mentions or reviews in *The Guardian* and *The Sunday Express* among others. *The Sunday Express* described it as: *"without doubt the most original book on the subject of smoking – and, more pertinently, what happens when you try to stop – ever published."* We have another 15-odd reviews lined up and probably another 20 looking very likely at this stage. Rich is being interviewed live on BBC Radio Scotland tomorrow.

So we were right about the fact that it's possible to get really good PR for new books from unknown publishers, and right about our ability to do it. I'm sure we were also right about going for quirky titles, as this seems to be what attracts the coverage.

And actually, I think going for non-book trade sales was the right decision. It's tough going, but it will pay off eventually. We'll find the outlets that *do* work – which I'm quite certain are there – and once we've found them we'll capitalise on them while most other publishers aren't even looking. Meantime people will become more accustomed to buying books outside bookshops. And when they do we'll be ready and waiting for them.

Perhaps the thing we were most right of all about was our editorial board, as we call them. Our advisors have been on hand constantly with advice on anything and everything we have asked, and have repeatedly come up with brilliant ideas and necessary forewarnings. They are always positive and enthusiastic, and I could not possibly overrate the contribution they have made to White Ladder.

Money

Things are tight, I'll be frank. In the long term we still reckon the prospects are excellent, but in the short term we have no money. We've put another £3,000 into the business and are living on royalties from books we've written for other publishers in the past. Our belts are almost as tight as they will go. Rich has written a couple of other books in the last year, but I've had time to write only one. Mind you, I have been paid between £150 and £300 for at least four articles I've written about *Kids & Co*.

We have a far clearer picture now of how the finances will pan out. We know what our average discount is now, and can be more realistic about sales. If we personally tighten our belts over the next year or so, things should improve considerably in 2005 when we're up to full speed.

We have also been very unlucky with our foreign rights sales. That is to say, we have had none at all. Our poor agent number four has had to give up – foreign rights aren't really his thing and he hasn't been going about it the right way. (He's still both my agent and Rich's as individuals, and a very good one.) However, almost all foreign rights deals are done at the Frankfurt Book Fair at the beginning of October, and we've just signed up a proper foreign rights agent who comes highly recommended and tells us we should expect substantial foreign rights on our first four books (which is how many she's taking to Frankfurt with her). That should mean a few thousand pounds at least, although it may take a few months to come through. This will mean that we won't need to put any more money into the business, and can even start thinking about paying back the money we've put in so far.

And about that BT compensation claim...

You may be wondering what became of all the shenanigans over BT and the compensation we wanted for losing our phones just as we launched the business. BT have an immensely complicated form you have to fill in for compensation, in which you have to answer any number of questions for which we had no answer. Questions about your usual level of sales income and the like, which are unanswerable if you've only just launched the business.

Rich explained patiently to BT that we were unable to complete the form, to which they responded that in that case they were unable to award compensation. Rich was asking for £900 for 'stress, nervous exhaustion, disappointment and frustration'. It's not the mechanical breakdown that's so upsetting – that can happen to any organisation – it's the complete lack of enthusiasm or practical action towards putting it right promptly. Had we been allowed to, we would happily just have claimed for time wasted showing endless engineers round the place when we should have been working. Sadly, that wasn't an option either. In fact, the BT system means that you can be messed about horrendously, as we were, and yet be unable to claim for more than a paltry few quid.

Anyway, in the end Rich became so hugely frustrated at BT's refusal to budge that he wrote to them complaining stiffly about our treatment, and playing the card that he had previously resisted using: the fact that I was keeping this journal with the intention of publishing it, and that our telephone problems would inevitably be included. I thought you might like to see the letter they sent in reply:

Dear Mr Craze

Re; compensation claim

Thank you for your letter of the 26 May 2003, regarding your claim for compensation and in reply to my letter of the 22 May 2003.

Firstly, may I refer you to my previous letter. The fifth paragraph advises that I appreciated your loss would be difficult to evidence and with that in mind, I asked you to submit a breakdown of how you had calculated your claimed loss at £900.00. You have now advised that this loss was solely for 'stress, nervous exhaustion, disappointment and frustration'.

Unfortunately and as previously advised, the Scheme is literally for Actual Financial Loss and makes no provision for stress, disappointment etc., as these cannot be quantified. To attempt to compensate for such things would be neither possible or practical. Believe me, I do understand your frustration with the service you received and do not wish to appear unsympathetic but wish to assist you in your claim but I cannot agree to your suggestion to pay compensation for this.

However, in an effort to be fair and reasonable and looking at your details again, I have found a way forward. Using your own calculation on the sheet marked 'Notes' as follows;

Assumed sales for each title, months 1-3 = 1,330 @ approx. £6.99 per title = £9,297.00 for the 3 months. Divided by 3 for an average month = £3,099.00.

Divided by 31 days in March 2003 = £100.00 per day x 9 days of BT liability = £900.00, the amount originally claimed.

As this was the amount originally claimed on the form, I am pleased to advise that I have arranged a cheque for this amount, in full and final settlement and this will reach you within 5-10 working days.

With regard to the 'White Ladder Diaries' and your last paragraph, I do sympathise with you and the problems you had and yes, I understand that you reserve the right to 'tell the world' if you feel you have been treated unfairly but must point out that BT also reserve the right to answer any criticism in the public domain.

Thank you for your patience and courtesy in this matter and I very much hope that any future contact with BT will be of a more positive nature.

Yours sincerely...

I think that shows that even BT can find a way to resolve these things if they have a mind to, and that it's always worth persisting. The actual amount we lost – in terms of work that never got done and everything else – is impossible to calculate (as BT pointed out). But at least we managed to establish a level of compensation that we didn't find insulting.

The future

You have to plan ahead in publishing, as in all industries, even when the future is slightly less certain than you might hope. We have 2004 planned out, and we have several projects in development for 2005. In fact, we've just commissioned our first author. We're also starting to plan our first charity book, for 2005, something we're both really keen to do. We'll cover the direct costs, pay the author a royalty, and donate all the rest of the profits to the charity.

Perhaps the most important thing of all for Rich and me is how
much fun we've had. We work longer hours than we can remember, often going back to work after the children have gone to bed,
but we don't begrudge a second of it. White Ladder has been such
an exhilarating project, and looks set to continue that way for
years to come. We're learning all the time – new skills, a new
industry – and that's what makes it so stimulating. Even if the
whole thing folded tomorrow, neither of us would regret doing it
for an instant. (Especially since we made sure that if it folds, we
don't go with it.) But if enthusiasm and effort count for anything,
White Ladder is here to stay.

If you're reading this book because you are launching – or have
recently launched – a new business, I wish you the best of luck. If
you are still thinking about whether or not to become your own
boss, I would urge you to do it. Go one step at a time, researching
all the way to make sure your idea is viable, and slowly building up
the momentum. You'll find that the fear evaporates once you get
going, and the stimulation of working for yourself and learning
new skills is wonderful. Give yourself a secure financial basis, so
that if it all falls apart you don't lose the house and everything else,
and then – if the research shows that your idea is sound – go for it.
You'll have such fun.

GOLDEN RULES

- *Get your ideas down on paper.* That way you can see them clearly. And you can always adapt them later; indeed you almost certainly will.

- *Don't just think about it – do something.* Talk to people, check out some facts and figures. This activity is what gives you the momentum to turn your idea from a pipe-dream into a reality.

- *Talk to everyone you can.* This is one big reason why it's an enormous help to start a business in an industry you already know about. But even if you have no contacts at all, you'll still find helpful people if you ask around.

- *Write your mission statement.* Do this early on because it will help you focus your mind on what exactly your new business is there for.

- *Write a business plan.* Even if you don't need to raise any funds and no one but you will ever see it, this process is invaluable for drawing your attention to all sorts of issues you need to think about. Over 90% of businesses that fail had no business plan.

- *Get your hands dirty.* No one but you can do your market research. It's your direct involvement in the details of research-ing and launching the business which will ensure its success.

- *Remember that your website is a big part of how you promote your brand.* If you need a website, build it into your initial design thinking. Don't add it later as an afterthought. Even if you can't afford to set it up now, you can still plan it.

- *You can't start a business without a proper cash flow forecast.*

- *Learn everything you can about your industry.*

- *Listen to your gut feeling.* It may not be right every time, but it often is. So you need to follow through your gut ideas and find out if they're really as unworkable as they may seem at first.

- *The smaller you are, the more professional you have to look.*
- *Keep it simple.* Don't waste money on fancy stationery and the like. Put what money you have into the product or your customer service, where it will actively encourage sales.
- *Set up and integrate your database right from the start.* If you're starting the kind of business where you're ever going to need a database, you need to find the money to get it in place from the start.
- *Beg or borrow if it saves you money.* If it doesn't affect the product and service you give your customers, don't spend money you don't have to.
- *Think hard about discounts, because you can't reduce them later.* If your business is going to sell to wholesalers or retailers, you'll need to get the discounts right from the start.
- *When it comes to website design, keep it simple.* It's that 'keep it simple' rule again. Unless you're in an industry where it's de rigeur, don't use fancy graphics and animations – they cost too much and people get fed up waiting for them to download.
- *Plan your PR well in advance.*
- *Contact journalists by phone as well as in writing.*
- *Think creatively about who your customers might be.*
- *Look ahead.* You have to juggle your current demands with the future demands of the business. If you focus entirely on the present, in a few weeks or months you'll suddenly find your business starting to fail.
- *Read everything relevant you can get your hands on.*
- *Get everything right from the start.* Even when it hardly shows – from branding to databases to your website – you can start small, but you must be on the right road from the outset.
- *Look after the details.* A brand is largely built on detail – as is good customer service, a high quality product and all the other things that matter.

- *Make contingency plans.* You have no idea at this stage what might happen, so think through the worst – or best – scenario and make sure you're prepared for coping with it.
- *You're not selling, you're offering a partnership.* If you find the prospect of hard selling daunting, remind yourself you're simply offering people a deal which will benefit them as well as you.
- *Keep your printing simple.* If you only pay for something simple, you can afford to do it smartly and well. Don't spend your budget on unnecessary colours or quantities, and then have to economise on quality.
- *Don't be afraid to ask.* You can't possibly know everything. If you're stumped, think who you know who can give you the answer, or at least point you in the right direction, and ask them.
- *Where all else is equal, aim to use smaller suppliers.* There may be other factors here but, if you have a choice of good suppliers, you'll get more empathy from fellow small businesses, and you'll be more important to them.
- *Don't be afraid to ask for endorsements.* The right person can add immense credibility to your product and people don't mind being asked. The worst they can do is politely decline, and you'd be surprised how many will say yes.
- *When you have to deal with bureaucracy, you can't beat persistence.* It's a matter of being dogged, finding the right person or system, and just sticking at it. It's worth it in the end.
- *When time is limited, work out the most cost-effective way to spend what time you have.*

Index

Index

  bookkeeping 162, 166–7
  cash flow forecasting 50–5
  Sage 70, 74, 75, 166
  VAT registration 56–7
address labels 151–2, 158
advisory panels 63–7
Allin, Mark 17–19, 27, 47, 55, 58, 70, 88, 122, 151, 195
  on branding 124, 126–7
  on discounts 96–7
  and the editorial board 174, 176
  on selling 139, 174
Alton Logistics 104–5, 140, 173
Amazon 1, 4, 14, 18, 44, 58
  online ordering through 32, 139–40
  sales through 185
  small publishers scheme 84–5, 172–3
Ball, Elie 1, 2, 7, 70, 78, 96, 110–11, 112, 120, 131, 151, 153–4, 177, 187
banking 35, 119, 143–4
  online 73–4
Bath Press 34, 46, 55
Bell, David 148
Bertrams 14, 74, 150–1, 195
book clubs 4, 18, 37, 133–4
The Book People 183
bookmarks 129–30
bookshops 4, 9, 11, 37, 194–5
  independents 37, 40, 71–2, 82, 178
  mailshots to 43–4
  payments by 35
  returns from 37–8, 38–9, 43
branding 10, 124, 126–8, 205
BT 68, 71, 75–6, 152, 154–5, 162, 163, 165, 168, 169, 170, 174–5
  Call Minder 135–6, 149, 159, 160, 163
  compensation claim 171–2, 190, 200–2
  and diverted lines 178
  TotalCare 175
  see also telephones
business cards 11
business outline 3–7
business plans 25–30, 31, 204

Capstone 10, 17–19, 122, 126, 127, 195
cash flow forecasting 50–5
charity books 2, 5
Clarke, Matthew 72, 82, 95, 137, 150, 178
Cleese, John 60, 115, 118, 137, 180
companies, selling Kids & Co to 88–9, 148, 164, 179–80, 183–4, 195
company ethos 5–6, 26
company structure 6–7
computer software 61–2
contingency plans 206
costings 14–15
  postage costs 161–2
  printing costs 15, 55, 145–7
  start-up 40–1, 68–9
Cotton, Bob 10
credit card transactions 45–6, 102–4, 119, 135, 142–3, 149, 165–6
customers
  database 61–2, 76–9, 134, 142, 153
  pack sent out to 177
  as salespeople 138–9, 141–2, 146, 148, 181–2, 196

Data Protection Register 35, 79, 118
debit card payments 102–4
discounts 32, 74, 76, 205
  Amazon 84–5, 140
  Bertrams 150
  calculating 93, 94, 96–7, 104–5, 196
  costings 14
distribution 8, 18, 34–5, 82–3
  flyers/leaflets 138–9, 141–2, 146, 148, 158–9, 161, 162–3
  independent distributors 9
  and readership 100
e-mails 99
  e-mailing press releases 131–2, 156–7, 167–8
  selected emailings 142–3
editorial board 7, 62–3, 80, 95, 174, 176, 182, 198–9
endorsements 170, 206
equity 13
foreign rights agents/sales 48, 49, 82, 87, 151, 155, 177, 186, 199–200

freelance journalists 106–10
future plans 202–3

Gardners 14, 82, 83, 137, 138, 147, 148, 173, 179, 195

Hayward, Mark 7–11, 30, 47–8, 82, 87, 95
Hill, Susan 31–8, 47, 105, 151
holidays 111–12
Horlick, Nicola 170
Howe, Graham 48–9, 69, 162
HSBC 73–4, 103, 119, 142–4

Independent Publisher's Guild (IPG) 18
insurance 85–6, 173
ISBN numbers 67, 68–9, 72–3, 80

journalists, freelance 106–10

Kids & Co
  changing titles 16, 45, 63
  contract 95
  cover design 58–60
  flyer/order form for 89–91
  foreign rights 82, 151
  media coverage 91, 97–8, 99, 117–18, 123, 125–6, 128–9, 130–3, 149, 170, 197–8
    local 171, 172, 178, 179, 182, 186
    radio 160, 186, 198
  media guides for 92
  payment for articles about 199
  bookshops 150, 178, 184, 185, 189
  companies 88–9, 148, 164, 179–80, 183–4, 195
  leaflet distributors 138–9, 141–2, 146, 148, 181–2, 196
  level of 173–4, 180, 188–9
  and parenting catalogues/websites 167–8, 172

If you like this book, how about earning a few bob recommending it to other people?

We're looking for people who would like to earn a bit of extra cash, or maybe fundraise for a favourite charity, by helping to sell *The White Ladder Diaries*, and our other books.

The deal's very simple. If you're interested, we'll send you a handful of leaflets with an order form on the back. All you have to do is to mark them with your name and hand them out. Give them to friends, leave them in shops… we'll give you a few ideas to get you started. No need to do any hard selling if you're not comfortable with that. Then, for every order that comes back with your name on, we pay you a healthy commission. It's as simple as that. When you're ready for more leaflets, we'll send them to you.

If you want to know more, call Richard on 01803 814124. We'd love you to join us.

Contact us

You're welcome to contact White Ladder Press if you have any questions or comments for either us or the author. Please use whichever of the following routes suits you.

Phone 01803 813343 between 9am and 5.30pm
Email enquiries@whiteladderpress.com
Fax 01803 813928
Address: White Ladder Press, Great Ambrook, Near Ipplepen, Devon TQ12 5UL
Website www.whiteladderpress.com

KIDS & Co

"Ros Jay has had a brilliant idea, and what is more she has executed it brilliantly. **KIDS & CO** is the essential handbook for any manager about to commit the act of parenthood, and a thoroughly entertaining read for everyone else" **JOHN CLEESE**

WHEN IT COMES TO RAISING YOUR KIDS, YOU KNOW MORE THAN YOU THINK.

So you spent five or ten years working before you started your family? Maybe more? Well, don't waste those hard-learned skills. Use them on your kids. Treat your children like customers, like employees, like colleagues.

No, really.

Just because you're a parent, your business skills don't have to go out of the window when you walk in through the front door. You may sometimes feel that the kids get the better of you every time, but here's one weapon you have that they don't: all those business skills you already have and they know nothing about. Closing the sale, win/win negotiating, motivational skills and all the rest.

Ros Jay is a professsional author who writes on both business and parenting topics, in this case simultaneously. She is the mother of three young children and stepmother to another three grown-up ones.

"The essential handbook for any manager about to commit the act of parenthood" JOHN CLEESE

KIDS & Co

Winning business tactics for every family

ROS JAY

THE VOICE OF TOBACCO

"An amazing new book on smoking – it has great style and humour, and is brilliantly funny. Read this happy smoker's guide – if only I had been the author." LESLIE PHILLIPS

What does the Voice of Tobacco say to you?
There's no need to give up; just cutting down will do.
How can it be bad for you when it feels so good?
Just one cigarette can't hurt you, now can it?

It's hard not to listen. Especially when, from the other side of the debate, we smokers have all been lectured by self-righteous prigs who think that (a) we should want to give up and (b) giving up smoking should be easy.

Well we don't and it ain't.

And yet there does come a time when, no matter how much we enjoy smoking, we have to become not smokers.

Richard Craze's guide gives it to you straight: what it's really like to give up smoking. The headaches, the sleepless-ness, the irritability. And The Voice. He's been there and his diary reports back from the front line. It may not be pleas-ant, but it's honest. It may or may not help you to give up smoking, but it will certainly get you looking at smoking in a new way. And it will give you some-thing to do with your hands.

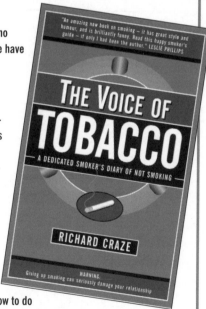

This is the diary of a dedicated and happy smoker who is now not smoking. Here's how he did it. Here's how to do it without the trauma, the withdrawal symptoms, the twitching, the bad temper. Yeah, right. In your dreams.

Order form

You can order any of our books via any of the contact routes on the previous page, including on our website. Or fill out the order form below and fax it or post it to us. We'll normally send your copy out by first class post within 24 hours (but please allow five days for delivery). We don't charge postage and packing.

Title (Mr/Mrs/Miss/Ms/Dr/Lord etc)

Name

Address

Postcode

Daytime phone number

Email

No. of copies	Title	Price	Total £
		TOTAL:	

Please either send us a cheque made out to White Ladder Press Ltd or fill in the credit card details below.

Type of card   ☐ Visa   ☐ Mastercard   ☐ Switch

Card number

Start date (if on card) _____ Expiry date _____ Issue no (Switch)_____

Name as shown on card

Signature